THIS

OR

THAT

Find Out How Well
You Know Each Other!

THIS

OR

THAT

1,500 QUESTIONS TO NURTURE CONNECTIONS
WITH FRIENDS & FAMILY

BETTER DAY BOOKS®

HAPPY · CREATIVE · CURATED

BETTER DAY BOOKS®

Better Day Books
P.O. Box 21462
York, PA 17402
Phone: 717-487-5523
Email: hello@betterdaybooks.com
www.betterdaybooks.com
@better_day_books

Schiffer Publishing
4880 Lower Valley Road
Atglen, PA 19310
Phone: 610-593-1777
Fax: 610-593-2002
Email: info@schifferbooks.com
www.schifferbooks.com

This title is available for promotional or commercial use,
including special editions. Contact info@schifferbooks.com
for more information.

Be silly.
Be honest.
Be kind.

—RALPH WALDO EMERSON

CONTENTS

> ## THE FUN DOESN'T STOP AT THE END OF THE QUIZZES!
>
> Check out the questions in the Tell Me More chapter to keep the conversation going.

INTRODUCTION

Welcome to This or That like you've never played it before! Inside this super-fun book, you will not only ask and answer creative "this or that" questions, but you will also have the opportunity to guess the other player's responses. If you predict the answers correctly, awesome! You know your friend very well. If not ... sorry, but you go to the back of the book to find more questions related to the theme that you and your friend can discuss together. It's the most fun way to strengthen friendships, build bonds, and get people talking to one another!

This creative version of the game is similar to other this-or-that games you might have played, but read the instructions on the next page before getting started so you can get the most out of this book ... and the experience!

> ### TIP: Keep Answers Secret
> The convenient flaps on this book can be used to conceal answers!

HERE'S HOW TO PLAY

CHOOSE ROLES:
Decide who will be Player 1 (predicting Player 2's answers) and who will be Player 2 (giving their own answers).

SELECT A QUIZ PAGE:
Player 1 browses the book and picks a quiz page.

PREDICT RESPONSES:
Player 1 first predicts Player 2's answers and fills out their side of the quiz.

READ AND RECORD:
Player 1 then reads each question and records Player 2's responses, filling out Player 2's side of the page. Alternatively, you can use the flap to cover up Player 1's predictions, and Player 2 can fill out their own answers directly in the book.

SCORE:
Using the checkboxes in the center of the page, tally up how many answers Player 1 predicted correctly! If they correctly predicted more than half of the answers, they can move on to a new quiz page. If not, they can turn to the back of the book for more questions to get to know Player 2 better!

Did you get more than half of your predictions wrong?

No worries! Go to the back of the book and find the associated chapter number. Then, ask your friend more questions on the topic so you can get to know them better.

1 Player 1 fills out this side with their predictions for Player 2's answers.

TIP! Use the flaps of the book to hide your guesses!

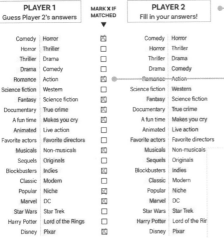

MOVIES & FILM

PLAYER 1 Guess Player 2's answers		MARK X IF MATCHED ▼	PLAYER 2 Fill in your answers!	
Comedy	Horror	☒	Comedy	Horror
Horror	Thriller	☐	Horror	Thriller
Thriller	Drama	☐	Thriller	Drama
Drama	Comedy	☐	Drama	Comedy
Romance	Action	☒	Romance	Action
Science fiction	Western	☐	Science fiction	Western
Fantasy	Science fiction	☒	Fantasy	Science fiction
Documentary	True crime	☒	Documentary	True crime
A fun time	Makes you cry	☒	A fun time	Makes you cry
Animated	Live action	☐	Animated	Live action
Favorite actors	Favorite directors	☐	Favorite actors	Favorite directors
Musicals	Non-musicals	☒	Musicals	Non-musicals
Sequels	Originals	☐	Sequels	Originals
Blockbusters	Indies	☒	Blockbusters	Indies
Classic	Modern	☐	Classic	Modern
Popular	Niche	☒	Popular	Niche
Marvel	DC	☒	Marvel	DC
Star Wars	Star Trek	☐	Star Wars	Star Trek
Harry Potter	Lord of the Rings	☐	Harry Potter	Lord of the Rir
Disney	Pixar	☒	Disney	Pixar

TOTAL MATCHED | 10 | **Get to know each other better! Go to page 119.**

2 Then, Player 2 marks their answers on this side.

3 Mark an X in the box if Player 1's prediction was right!

4 Tally up the score at the bottom!

5 Did you correctly predict a lot of responses? Great! If not, go to the back of the book to learn more about each other.

TELL ME MORE ◊ MEDIA

44 BOOKS
- What kind of book would you love to write?
- What are the top three books you've ever read?
- What book world would you love to visit?

45 ART
- What kind (or kinds) of art do you think you are good at?
- Do you notice art in everyday life? Where and when?
- How much would you spend for a painting that you loved?

46 MOVIES & FILM
- What job would you prefer to have in making a movie?
- What is your all-time favorite movie or movie franchise?
- Who are your favorite actors and actresses?

47 MOVIE TIME
- How often do you watch a movie in a theater?
- Do you prefer director's cuts or theatrical versions?
- What snack do you wish you could sneak into a movie theater?

48 SOCIAL MEDIA
- Which social media site do you spend the most time on?
- Which social media site do you enjoy using the most?
- Do you think you have a healthy relationship with social media?

49 TELEVISION
- What is your all-time favorite television series?
- What is the last television show you completed?
- What story do you wish would be adapted into a show?

50 VIDEO GAMES
- What is the coolest video game you've ever played?
- What game did you fail to beat, despite your best efforts?
- What game do you think is totally overrated?

51 BOARD GAMES
- What board game do you always suggest to play?
- Are you best at word games, puzzle games, or something else?
- What board game do you think would be cool as a movie?

CHAPTER 1

HAPPY HOBBIES

In this chapter you will find a series of questions designed to delve into your hobbies and interests. Find out whether the players love an indie rock festival in an open field or blaring dance music in a crowded club, who likes solo sports or team sports, and more.

Let's get started!

DO MORE OF WHATEVER
MAKES YOUR SOUL HAPPY.

MUSIC MANIA

PLAYER 1		MARK X IF	PLAYER 2	
Guess Player 2's answers		MATCHED ▼	**Fill in your answers!**	
Acoustic	Electric	☐	Acoustic	Electric
Ballads	Beats	☐	Ballads	Beats
Blasting	Background	☐	Blasting	Background
Classic rock	Heavy metal	☐	Classic rock	Heavy metal
Festival	Stadium	☐	Festival	Stadium
Front row	Backstage	☐	Front row	Backstage
Guitar	Bass	☐	Guitar	Bass
Headphones	Speakers	☐	Headphones	Speakers
Indie	Pop	☐	Indie	Pop
Live music	DJ	☐	Live music	DJ
Love songs	Anthems	☐	Love songs	Anthems
Original	Remix	☐	Original	Remix
Packed club	Coffeehouse	☐	Packed club	Coffeehouse
Playlist	Shuffle	☐	Playlist	Shuffle
Sing-alongs	Solos	☐	Sing-alongs	Solos
Sit	Dance	☐	Sit	Dance
Vinyl	Streaming	☐	Vinyl	Streaming
Chill beats	Fast songs	☐	Chill beats	Fast songs
Radio	Albums	☐	Radio	Albums
Vocals	Instrumental	☐	Vocals	Instrumental

TOTAL MATCHED ____ ☐

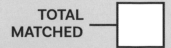

Get to know each other better! Go to page 116.

HOBBY TIME

PLAYER 2 — Fill in your answers!		MARK X IF MATCHED ▼	PLAYER 1 — Guess Player 2's answers	
Ice skating	Inline skating	☐	Ice skating	Inline skating
Painting	Pottery	☐	Painting	Pottery
Acting	Singing	☐	Acting	Singing
Photography	Graphic design	☐	Photography	Graphic design
Puzzles	Word searches	☐	Puzzles	Word searches
Music	Podcasts	☐	Music	Podcasts
Makeup	Hairstyling	☐	Makeup	Hairstyling
Cooking	Baking	☐	Cooking	Baking
Drawing	Coloring	☐	Drawing	Coloring
Video games	Board games	☐	Video games	Board games
Hiking	Camping	☐	Hiking	Camping
YouTube	Filmmaking	☐	YouTube	Filmmaking
Writing	Reading	☐	Writing	Reading
Knitting	Sewing	☐	Knitting	Sewing
Songwriting	Playing instruments	☐	Songwriting	Playing instruments
Gardening	Woodworking	☐	Gardening	Woodworking
Card games	Chess	☐	Card games	Chess
Hula hoop	Jump rope	☐	Hula hoop	Jump rope
Scrapbooking	Origami	☐	Scrapbooking	Origami
Friendship bracelets	Tie-dye	☐	Friendship bracelets	Tie-dye

TOTAL MATCHED ⬚

Get to know each other better! Go to page 116.

ATHLETICS

PLAYER 1 — Guess Player 2's answers		MARK **X** IF MATCHED ▼	PLAYER 2 — Fill in your answers!	
Running	Walking	☐	Running	Walking
Football	Basketball	☐	Football	Basketball
Baseball	Lacrosse	☐	Baseball	Lacrosse
Ballet	Hip-hop	☐	Ballet	Hip-hop
Soccer	Tennis	☐	Soccer	Tennis
Golf	Bowling	☐	Golf	Bowling
Frisbee	Handball	☐	Frisbee	Handball
Hockey	Volleyball	☐	Hockey	Volleyball
Cheerleading	Dance	☐	Cheerleading	Dance
Bike	Scooter	☐	Bike	Scooter
Trampoline	Rock climbing	☐	Trampoline	Rock climbing
Sports on TV	Sports in person	☐	Sports on TV	Sports in person
Skiing	Snowboarding	☐	Skiing	Snowboarding
Wrestling	Boxing	☐	Wrestling	Boxing
Jump rope	Hula-Hoop	☐	Jump rope	Hula-Hoop
Yoga	Pilates	☐	Yoga	Pilates
Push-ups	Sit-ups	☐	Push-ups	Sit-ups
Surfing	Boogie boarding	☐	Surfing	Boogie boarding
Darts	Archery	☐	Darts	Archery
Team sports	Individual sports	☐	Team sports	Individual sports

TOTAL MATCHED ☐

Get to know each other better! Go to page 116.

EXTRACURRICULARS

PLAYER 2		MARK **X** IF MATCHED ▼	PLAYER 1	
PLAYER 2 Fill in your answers!			**PLAYER 1** Guess Player 2's answers	
Art club	Debate club	☐	Art club	Debate club
Science club	Business club	☐	Science club	Business club
Soccer	Field hockey	☐	Soccer	Field hockey
Cheerleading	Dance	☐	Cheerleading	Dance
Yoga	Martial arts	☐	Yoga	Martial arts
Chess club	Video game club	☐	Chess club	Video game club
Marching band	Theater	☐	Marching band	Theater
Robotics club	Choir	☐	Robotics club	Choir
Photography club	Hiking club	☐	Photography club	Hiking club
Cooking club	Yearbook	☐	Cooking club	Yearbook
Wrestling	Track and field	☐	Wrestling	Track and field
Writing club	Color guard	☐	Writing club	Color guard
Environmental club	Swim team	☐	Environmental club	Swim team
Honor society	Marching band	☐	Honor society	Marching band
Baseball	Cross-country	☐	Baseball	Cross-country
School newspaper	A.M. announcements	☐	School newspaper	A.M. announcements
Student government	Young professionals	☐	Student government	Young professionals
Jazz band	Orchestra	☐	Jazz band	Orchestra
School mascot	Class president	☐	School mascot	Class president
Hallway monitor	Tutor	☐	Hallway monitor	Tutor

TOTAL MATCHED — ☐

Get to know each other better! Go to page 116.

TECH & GADGETS

PLAYER 1 — Guess Player 2's answers		MARK X IF MATCHED ▼	PLAYER 2 — Fill in your answers!	
Apple	Android	☐	Apple	Android
PC	Mac	☐	PC	Mac
Chromebook	Tablet	☐	Chromebook	Tablet
Smartphone	Flip phone	☐	Smartphone	Flip phone
Headphones	Earbuds	☐	Headphones	Earbuds
Bluetooth	Wired	☐	Bluetooth	Wired
Keyboard	Mouse	☐	Keyboard	Mouse
Desktop	Laptop	☐	Desktop	Laptop
Phone camera	DSLR camera	☐	Phone camera	DSLR camera
Fitbit	Apple Watch	☐	Fitbit	Apple Watch
Gaming PC	Gaming console	☐	Gaming PC	Gaming console
Amazon Echo	Google Home	☐	Amazon Echo	Google Home
Kindle	Nook	☐	Kindle	Nook
Electric toothbrush	Electric flosser	☐	Electric toothbrush	Electric flosser
Air fryer	Toaster oven	☐	Air fryer	Toaster oven
Keurig	Nespresso	☐	Keurig	Nespresso
Big hard drive	Cloud storage	☐	Big hard drive	Cloud storage
Photo printer	Printing service	☐	Photo printer	Printing service
Smart lightbulbs	Smart TV	☐	Smart lightbulbs	Smart TV
Wireless charging	Plug-in charging	☐	Wireless charging	Plug-in charging

TOTAL MATCHED — ☐

Get to know each other better! Go to page 116.

ENTERTAINMENT

PLAYER 2 — Fill in your answers!		MARK **X** IF MATCHED ▼	PLAYER 1 — Guess Player 2's answers	
Physical book	Audiobook	☐	Physical book	Audiobook
Board game	Card game	☐	Board game	Card game
Play	Concert	☐	Play	Concert
Museum trip	Art gallery visit	☐	Museum trip	Art gallery visit
Amusement park	Water park	☐	Amusement park	Water park
Mini-golf	Driving range	☐	Mini-golf	Driving range
Bowling	Laser tag	☐	Bowling	Laser tag
Comedy show	Magic show	☐	Comedy show	Magic show
Jigsaw puzzle	Crossword puzzle	☐	Jigsaw puzzle	Crossword puzzle
Sudoku	Word search	☐	Sudoku	Word search
Play an instrument	Sing	☐	Play an instrument	Sing
Sporting event	Concert	☐	Sporting event	Concert
Aquarium	Zoo	☐	Aquarium	Zoo
Book club	Exercise class	☐	Book club	Exercise class
Yoga	Hiking	☐	Yoga	Hiking
Escape room	Haunted house	☐	Escape room	Haunted house
Watch TV	Watch YouTube	☐	Watch TV	Watch YouTube
Craft	Cook	☐	Craft	Cook
City stroll	Country walk	☐	City stroll	Country walk
Roller coaster	Ferris wheel	☐	Roller coaster	Ferris wheel

TOTAL MATCHED ⎯ ☐

Get to know each other better! Go to page 116.

SHOPPING

PLAYER 1		MARK X IF MATCHED ▼	PLAYER 2	
PLAYER 1 Guess Player 2's answers			**PLAYER 2** Fill in your answers!	
Online	In-store	☐	Online	In-store
Credit	Debit	☐	Credit	Debit
Cash	Card	☐	Cash	Card
Clearance	New arrivals	☐	Clearance	New arrivals
Boutique	Department	☐	Boutique	Department
Brand-name	Generic	☐	Brand-name	Generic
Mall	Downtown	☐	Mall	Downtown
Shoes	Clothes	☐	Shoes	Clothes
Accessories	Jewelry	☐	Accessories	Jewelry
Bargain	Luxe	☐	Bargain	Luxe
Thrift	New	☐	Thrift	New
Window-shopping	Buying	☐	Window-shopping	Buying
Grocery store	Convenience store	☐	Grocery store	Convenience store
Prepackaged	Self-service	☐	Prepackaged	Self-service
Supermarket	Farmer's market	☐	Supermarket	Farmer's market
Paper	Plastic	☐	Paper	Plastic
Shopaholic	Frugal	☐	Shopaholic	Frugal
Shop alone	Shop with friends	☐	Shop alone	Shop with friends
Shopping cart	Shopping basket	☐	Shopping cart	Shopping basket
Shop for fun	Shop for necessity	☐	Shop for fun	Shop for necessity

TOTAL MATCHED — ☐

Get to know each other better! Go to page 116.

OUTDOOR FUN

PLAYER 2 — Fill in your answers!		MARK **X** IF MATCHED ▼	PLAYER 1 — Guess Player 2's answers	
Picnic	Barbecue	☐	Picnic	Barbecue
Walking tour	Bicycle tour	☐	Walking tour	Bicycle tour
Nature hike	Birdwatching	☐	Nature hike	Birdwatching
Botanical garden	Zoo	☐	Botanical garden	Zoo
Historic site	Natural landmark	☐	Historic site	Natural landmark
Outdoor movie	Theater in the park	☐	Outdoor movie	Theater in the park
Music festival	Food festival	☐	Music festival	Food festival
Farmer's market	Flea market	☐	Farmer's market	Flea market
Apple picking	Pumpkin picking	☐	Apple picking	Pumpkin picking
Outdoor yoga	Relaxing walk	☐	Outdoor yoga	Relaxing walk
Stargazing	Night swim	☐	Stargazing	Night swim
Camping	Glamping	☐	Camping	Glamping
Hot-air balloon	Helicopter	☐	Hot-air balloon	Helicopter
Whale watching	Swim with dolphins	☐	Whale watching	Swim with dolphins
Kayak tour	River cruise	☐	Kayak tour	River cruise
Horseback riding	Carriage ride	☐	Horseback riding	Carriage ride
Snorkeling	Glass-bottom boat	☐	Snorkeling	Glass-bottom boat
Scenic drive	Motorcycle ride	☐	Scenic drive	Motorcycle ride
Saltwater fishing	Freshwater fishing	☐	Saltwater fishing	Freshwater fishing
Mountain biking	Road cycling	☐	Mountain biking	Road cycling

TOTAL MATCHED — ☐

Get to know each other better! Go to page 116.

CHAPTER 2

FOOD & DRINK

Food: we can't live without it—but then again, why would we want to? Take a journey through every meal and all your favorite dishes, toppings, ingredients, and drinks. Do you go for sushi or ramen? Do you prefer soft-serve or hand-scooped ice cream? Is hot and spicy your jam?

It's time to chow down and find out!

IN A WORLD FULL OF
MUFFINS, BE A CUPCAKE.

FOOD FAVES

PLAYER 1 Guess Player 2's answers	MARK X IF MATCHED ▼	PLAYER 2 Fill in your answers!
Sweet : Savory	☐	Sweet : Savory
Sour : Spicy	☐	Sour : Spicy
Peanut butter : Nutella	☐	Peanut butter : Nutella
Whipped cream : Syrup	☐	Whipped cream : Syrup
Berries : Bananas	☐	Berries : Bananas
Cereal : Oatmeal	☐	Cereal : Oatmeal
Butter : Cream cheeses	☐	Butter : Cream cheeses
Lemonade : Fruit punch	☐	Lemonade : Fruit punch
Ice cream : Italian ice	☐	Ice cream : Italian ice
Bagel : Toast	☐	Bagel : Toast
Rainbow sprinkles : Chocolate sprinkles	☐	Rainbow sprinkles : Chocolate sprinkles
Bubble gum : Mints	☐	Bubble gum : Mints
Peanut butter : Jelly	☐	Peanut butter : Jelly
Fake meat : Tofu	☐	Fake meat : Tofu
Fork and spoon : Chopsticks	☐	Fork and spoon : Chopsticks
Well done : Rare	☐	Well done : Rare
Crispy : Chewy	☐	Crispy : Chewy
Peeled fruit : Skin on	☐	Peeled fruit : Skin on
Garlic : Onions	☐	Garlic : Onions
Food touching : Food separated	☐	Food touching : Food separated

TOTAL MATCHED — ☐

Get to know each other better! Go to page 117.

BREAKFAST

PLAYER 2 Fill in your answers!	MARK X IF MATCHED ▼	PLAYER 1 Guess Player 2's answers
Bacon : Sausage	☐	Bacon : Sausage
Bagel : English muffin	☐	Bagel : English muffin
Eat alone : Eat with company	☐	Eat alone : Eat with company
Eat in bed : Eat at the table	☐	Eat in bed : Eat at the table
Only in the morning : Anytime	☐	Only in the morning : Anytime
Brunch : Breakfast	☐	Brunch : Breakfast
Coffee : Tea	☐	Coffee : Tea
Donuts : Muffins	☐	Donuts : Muffins
Just a little syrup : The whole bottle	☐	Just a little syrup : The whole bottle
On the go : At home	☐	On the go : At home
Orange juice : Apple juice	☐	Orange juice : Apple juice
Pancakes : Waffles	☐	Pancakes : Waffles
Read the cereal box : Scroll your phone	☐	Read the cereal box : Scroll your phone
Scrambled eggs : Fried eggs	☐	Scrambled eggs : Fried eggs
In your PJs : After a shower	☐	In your PJs : After a shower
Bacon and eggs : Avocado toast	☐	Bacon and eggs : Avocado toast
Egg white omelet : Meat lover's omelet	☐	Egg white omelet : Meat lover's omelet
Café mocha : Fruit smoothie	☐	Café mocha : Fruit smoothie
Make from scratch : Microwave	☐	Make from scratch : Microwave
Hash browns : Grits	☐	Hash browns : Grits

TOTAL MATCHED — ☐

Get to know each other better! Go to page 117.

LUNCH

<table>
<tr><td colspan="2">PLAYER 1
Guess Player 2's answers</td><td>MARK X IF
MATCHED
▼</td><td colspan="2">PLAYER 2
Fill in your answers!</td></tr>
<tr><td>Soup</td><td>Salad</td><td>☐</td><td>Soup</td><td>Salad</td></tr>
<tr><td>White bread</td><td>Multigrain bread</td><td>☐</td><td>White bread</td><td>Multigrain bread</td></tr>
<tr><td>Turkey sandwich</td><td>Chicken sandwich</td><td>☐</td><td>Turkey sandwich</td><td>Chicken sandwich</td></tr>
<tr><td>Cheddar cheese</td><td>American cheese</td><td>☐</td><td>Cheddar cheese</td><td>American cheese</td></tr>
<tr><td>Wrap</td><td>Sandwich</td><td>☐</td><td>Wrap</td><td>Sandwich</td></tr>
<tr><td>School lunch</td><td>Packed lunch</td><td>☐</td><td>School lunch</td><td>Packed lunch</td></tr>
<tr><td>Roast beef</td><td>Ham</td><td>☐</td><td>Roast beef</td><td>Ham</td></tr>
<tr><td>Tomato soup</td><td>Chicken noodle soup</td><td>☐</td><td>Tomato soup</td><td>Chicken noodle soup</td></tr>
<tr><td>Caesar salad</td><td>Greek salad</td><td>☐</td><td>Caesar salad</td><td>Greek salad</td></tr>
<tr><td>Chicken salad</td><td>Tuna salad</td><td>☐</td><td>Chicken salad</td><td>Tuna salad</td></tr>
<tr><td>Sourdough</td><td>Brioche</td><td>☐</td><td>Sourdough</td><td>Brioche</td></tr>
<tr><td>Crunchy PB</td><td>Creamy PB</td><td>☐</td><td>Crunchy PB</td><td>Creamy PB</td></tr>
<tr><td>Grape jelly</td><td>Raspberry jelly</td><td>☐</td><td>Grape jelly</td><td>Raspberry jelly</td></tr>
<tr><td>Sub</td><td>Panini</td><td>☐</td><td>Sub</td><td>Panini</td></tr>
<tr><td>Grilled cheese</td><td>BLT</td><td>☐</td><td>Grilled cheese</td><td>BLT</td></tr>
<tr><td>Creamy soup</td><td>Non-creamy soup</td><td>☐</td><td>Creamy soup</td><td>Non-creamy soup</td></tr>
<tr><td>Italian roll</td><td>French baguette</td><td>☐</td><td>Italian roll</td><td>French baguette</td></tr>
<tr><td>Sloppy joes</td><td>Mac and cheese</td><td>☐</td><td>Sloppy joes</td><td>Mac and cheese</td></tr>
<tr><td>Fish sticks</td><td>Mozzarella sticks</td><td>☐</td><td>Fish sticks</td><td>Mozzarella sticks</td></tr>
<tr><td>Crust-off sandwiches</td><td>Crust-on sandwiches</td><td>☐</td><td>Crust-off sandwiches</td><td>Crust-on sandwiches</td></tr>
</table>

TOTAL MATCHED ☐

Get to know each other better! Go to page 117.

DINNER

PLAYER 2		MARK X IF	PLAYER 1	
Fill in your answers!		**MATCHED** ▼	**Guess Player 2's answers**	
Eat out	Stay in	☐	Eat out	Stay in
Pizza	Pasta	☐	Pizza	Pasta
Burger	Hot dog	☐	Burger	Hot dog
Chicken parmesan	Eggplant parmesan	☐	Chicken parmesan	Eggplant parmesan
Pasta with sauce	Pasta with butter	☐	Pasta with sauce	Pasta with butter
Cheeseburger	Plain burger	☐	Cheeseburger	Plain burger
Classic slice	Sicilian slice	☐	Classic slice	Sicilian slice
Mac and cheese	Lasagna	☐	Mac and cheese	Lasagna
Steak	Meatloaf	☐	Steak	Meatloaf
Hard-shell tacos	Soft-shell tacos	☐	Hard-shell tacos	Soft-shell tacos
Spaghetti	Penne	☐	Spaghetti	Penne
Sushi	Ramen	☐	Sushi	Ramen
Homemade pizza	Takeout pizza	☐	Homemade pizza	Takeout pizza
Italian food	Chinese food	☐	Italian food	Chinese food
Tacos	Quesadillas	☐	Tacos	Quesadillas
Egg roll	Spring roll	☐	Egg roll	Spring roll
Baked ziti	Penne alla vodka	☐	Baked ziti	Penne alla vodka
Shrimp tacos	Fish tacos	☐	Shrimp tacos	Fish tacos
Crispy chicken	Grilled chicken	☐	Crispy chicken	Grilled chicken
Classic burrito	Burrito bowl	☐	Classic burrito	Burrito bowl

TOTAL MATCHED ☐ — **Get to know each other better! Go to page 117.**

DESSERT

PLAYER 1 Guess Player 2's answers		MARK **X** IF MATCHED ▼	PLAYER 2 Fill in your answers!	
Cake	Cupcake	☐	Cake	Cupcake
Chocolate	Vanilla	☐	Chocolate	Vanilla
Ice cream	Frozen yogurt	☐	Ice cream	Frozen yogurt
Sundae	Milkshake	☐	Sundae	Milkshake
Chocolate chip	Gingerbread	☐	Chocolate chip	Gingerbread
Glazed donut	Frosted donut	☐	Glazed donut	Frosted donut
Ice cream cake	Regular cake	☐	Ice cream cake	Regular cake
Donuts	Donut holes	☐	Donuts	Donut holes
Pie	Cake	☐	Pie	Cake
Cookie dough	Cookies & cream	☐	Cookie dough	Cookies & cream
Snickerdoodle	Oatmeal cookie	☐	Snickerdoodle	Oatmeal cookie
Cherry	Blue raspberry	☐	Cherry	Blue raspberry
Dark chocolate	Milk chocolate	☐	Dark chocolate	Milk chocolate
Cup	Cone	☐	Cup	Cone
Soft-serve	Hand-scooped	☐	Soft-serve	Hand-scooped
Sour gummies	Non-sour gummies	☐	Sour gummies	Non-sour gummies
Brownies	Cookies	☐	Brownies	Cookies
Sherbet	Gelato	☐	Sherbet	Gelato
Ice pop	Italian ice	☐	Ice pop	Italian ice
Ice cream bar	Ice cream sandwich	☐	Ice cream bar	Ice cream sandwich

TOTAL MATCHED — ☐

Get to know each other better! Go to page 117.

SIDE DISHES

PLAYER 2 Fill in your answers!		MARK **X** IF MATCHED ▼	PLAYER 1 Guess Player 2's answers	
Sweet-potato fries	Regular fries	☐	Sweet-potato fries	Regular fries
Waffle fries	Curly fries	☐	Waffle fries	Curly fries
Crinkle-cut fries	Potato wedges	☐	Crinkle-cut fries	Potato wedges
Baked potatoes	Mashed potatoes	☐	Baked potatoes	Mashed potatoes
Green beans	Snap peas	☐	Green beans	Snap peas
White rice	Fried rice	☐	White rice	Fried rice
Bacon	Sausage	☐	Bacon	Sausage
Black beans	Baked beans	☐	Black beans	Baked beans
Fruit salad	Roasted veggies	☐	Fruit salad	Roasted veggies
Asparagus	Brussels sprouts	☐	Asparagus	Brussels sprouts
Potato salad	Coleslaw	☐	Potato salad	Coleslaw
Biscuits	Garlic bread	☐	Biscuits	Garlic bread
Cornbread	Dinner roll	☐	Cornbread	Dinner roll
Canned corn	Corn on the cob	☐	Canned corn	Corn on the cob
Mushrooms	Carrots	☐	Mushrooms	Carrots
Macaroni salad	Pickles	☐	Macaroni salad	Pickles
Zucchini	Eggplant	☐	Zucchini	Eggplant
Broccoli	Cauliflower	☐	Broccoli	Cauliflower
Onion rings	Tater Tots	☐	Onion rings	Tater Tots
Breadsticks	Garlic knots	☐	Breadsticks	Garlic knots

TOTAL MATCHED ——— ☐

Get to know each other better! Go to page 117.

SNACKS

PLAYER 1 — Guess Player 2's answers			PLAYER 2 — Fill in your answers!	
Chips	Pretzels	☐	Chips	Pretzels
Salty snacks	Sweet snacks	☐	Salty snacks	Sweet snacks
Tortilla chips	Potato chips	☐	Tortilla chips	Potato chips
Salt & vinegar chips	Ranch chips	☐	Salt & vinegar chips	Ranch chips
Popcorn	Crackers	☐	Popcorn	Crackers
Granola bars	Trail mix	☐	Granola bars	Trail mix
Veggie straws	Pita chips	☐	Veggie straws	Pita chips
Cheese curls	Cheese balls	☐	Cheese curls	Cheese balls
Peanuts	Cashews	☐	Peanuts	Cashews
Soft pretzels	Hard pretzels	☐	Soft pretzels	Hard pretzels
Baby carrots	Celery sticks	☐	Baby carrots	Celery sticks
Apple and PB	Cheese and crackers	☐	Apple and PB	Cheese and crackers
Carrots and ranch	Carrots and hummus	☐	Carrots and ranch	Carrots and hummus
Cheddar popcorn	Kettle corn	☐	Cheddar popcorn	Kettle corn
Wavy chips	Regular chips	☐	Wavy chips	Regular chips
BBQ chips	Spicy chips	☐	BBQ chips	Spicy chips
Fruit snacks	Mini cookies	☐	Fruit snacks	Mini cookies
Pretzel sticks	Mini pretzels	☐	Pretzel sticks	Mini pretzels
Chips and salsa	Chips and guac	☐	Chips and salsa	Chips and guac
Fresh fruit	Dried fruit	☐	Fresh fruit	Dried fruit

TOTAL MATCHED ____

Get to know each other better! Go to page 117.

BEVERAGES

PLAYER 2		MARK **X** IF MATCHED ▼	**PLAYER 1**	
Fill in your answers!			Guess Player 2's answers	
Coffee	Tea	☐	Coffee	Tea
Hot chocolate	Chai latte	☐	Hot chocolate	Chai latte
Soda	Lemonade	☐	Soda	Lemonade
Smoothie	Juice	☐	Smoothie	Juice
Iced coffee	Iced tea	☐	Iced coffee	Iced tea
Milkshake	Frappuccino	☐	Milkshake	Frappuccino
Sparkling water	Still water	☐	Sparkling water	Still water
Kombucha	Coconut water	☐	Kombucha	Coconut water
Green tea	Herbal tea	☐	Green tea	Herbal tea
Orange juice	Apple juice	☐	Orange juice	Apple juice
Cranberry juice	Grape juice	☐	Cranberry juice	Grape juice
Chocolate milk	Strawberry milk	☐	Chocolate milk	Strawberry milk
Energy drink	Sports drink	☐	Energy drink	Sports drink
Cappuccino	Macchiato	☐	Cappuccino	Macchiato
Ginger ale	Root beer	☐	Ginger ale	Root beer
Iced matcha	Iced latte	☐	Iced matcha	Iced latte
Lemon water	Cucumber water	☐	Lemon water	Cucumber water
Peach tea	Raspberry tea	☐	Peach tea	Raspberry tea
Hot apple cider	Hot chocolate	☐	Hot apple cider	Hot chocolate
Bubble tea	Mint tea	☐	Bubble tea	Mint tea

TOTAL MATCHED ⎯ ☐

Get to know each other better! Go to page 117.

CHAPTER 3

ME, MYSELF & I

This chapter digs deep into what makes you tick. You'll talk about your habits (good and bad!), imagine your futures, discover what gives you the shivers, and find out who's a teacher's pet and who's always ending up in the principal's office.

Let's learn more about each other.

THE BRAVEST THING YOU
CAN BE IS YOURSELF.

ALL ABOUT ME

PLAYER 1		MARK X IF MATCHED ▼	PLAYER 2	
Guess Player 2's answers			Fill in your answers!	
Introvert	Extrovert	☐	Introvert	Extrovert
Plan ahead	Go with the flow	☐	Plan ahead	Go with the flow
Morning person	Night owl	☐	Morning person	Night owl
Adventurous	Cautious	☐	Adventurous	Cautious
Analytical	Creative	☐	Analytical	Creative
Center of attention	Blending in	☐	Center of attention	Blending in
Leader	Follower	☐	Leader	Follower
Big-picture thinker	Detail-oriented	☐	Big-picture thinker	Detail-oriented
Spontaneous	Methodical	☐	Spontaneous	Methodical
Consistency	Change	☐	Consistency	Change
Logical	Emotional	☐	Logical	Emotional
Ambitious	Content	☐	Ambitious	Content
Optimist	Realist	☐	Optimist	Realist
Independent	Collaborative	☐	Independent	Collaborative
Empathetic	Objective	☐	Empathetic	Objective
Risk taker	Risk-averse	☐	Risk taker	Risk-averse
Open-minded	Opinionated	☐	Open-minded	Opinionated
Routine	Variety	☐	Routine	Variety
Problem solver	Listener	☐	Problem solver	Listener
Confident	Humble	☐	Confident	Humble

TOTAL MATCHED — ☐

Get to know each other better! Go to page 118.

HABITS

PLAYER 2		MARK X IF	PLAYER 1	
Fill in your answers!		**MATCHED** ▼	**Guess Player 2's answers**	
Books	YouTube	☐	Books	YouTube
Wake up early	Wake up late	☐	Wake up early	Wake up late
Morning shower	Evening shower	☐	Morning shower	Evening shower
Make bed	Leave bed unmade	☐	Make bed	Leave bed unmade
Floss teeth	Just brush teeth	☐	Floss teeth	Just brush teeth
Homework ASAP	Homework at night	☐	Homework ASAP	Homework at night
Handwritten notes	Digital notes	☐	Handwritten notes	Digital notes
Save money	Spend money	☐	Save money	Spend money
Dress up	Dress down	☐	Dress up	Dress down
Exercise daily	Nap daily	☐	Exercise daily	Nap daily
Messy room	Clean room	☐	Messy room	Clean room
Plan your week	Go with the flow	☐	Plan your week	Go with the flow
Study with friends	Study alone	☐	Study with friends	Study alone
Play sports	Do yoga	☐	Play sports	Do yoga
Video call	Chat	☐	Video call	Chat
Phone alarm	Clock alarm	☐	Phone alarm	Clock alarm
Slouching	Sitting up straight	☐	Slouching	Sitting up straight
Snack mindlessly	Snack in portions	☐	Snack mindlessly	Snack in portions
Gratitude journal	Dream journal	☐	Gratitude journal	Dream journal
Clean regularly	Clean when messy	☐	Clean regularly	Clean when messy

TOTAL MATCHED ⬚

Get to know each other better! Go to page 118.

CHILDHOOD NOSTALGIA

PLAYER 1		MARK **X** IF	PLAYER 2	
Guess Player 2's answers		MATCHED ▼	Fill in your answers!	
Crafts	Sports	☐	Crafts	Sports
The Wiggles	*Sesame Street*	☐	*The Wiggles*	*Sesame Street*
Jump rope	Hula-Hoop	☐	Jump rope	Hula-Hoop
Friendship bracelets	Hair braiding	☐	Friendship bracelets	Hair braiding
LEGOs	Nerf	☐	LEGOs	Nerf
Slip 'N Slide	Sprinkler	☐	Slip 'N Slide	Sprinkler
Fruit Roll-Ups	Goldfish	☐	Fruit Roll-Ups	Goldfish
Lunchables	PB&J	☐	Lunchables	PB&J
Sandcastle	Mud pie	☐	Sandcastle	Mud pie
Bikes	Bounce house	☐	Bikes	Bounce house
Candyland	Chutes and Ladders	☐	Candyland	Chutes and Ladders
Spin the bottle	Truth or dare	☐	Spin the bottle	Truth or dare
Razor scooter	Skateboard	☐	Razor scooter	Skateboard
Beanie Babies	Pokémon cards	☐	Beanie Babies	Pokémon cards
Polly Pocket	Barbie	☐	Polly Pocket	Barbie
Finger painting	Face painting	☐	Finger painting	Face painting
Lemonade stand	Car wash	☐	Lemonade stand	Car wash
Boardwalk	Carnival	☐	Boardwalk	Carnival
Hide-and-seek	Tag	☐	Hide-and-seek	Tag
Video games	Books	☐	Video games	Books

TOTAL MATCHED ____ ☐

Get to know each other better! Go to page 118.

SCHOOL

PLAYER 2 — Fill in your answers!	MARK X IF MATCHED ▼	PLAYER 1 — Guess Player 2's answers
Pen : Pencil	☐	Pen : Pencil
Big class : Small class	☐	Big class : Small class
Math : English	☐	Math : English
Science : History	☐	Science : History
Reading : Writing	☐	Reading : Writing
Art : Music	☐	Art : Music
Multiple choice : Free response	☐	Multiple choice : Free response
Mechanical pencil : Regular pencil	☐	Mechanical pencil : Regular pencil
Red pen : Blue pen	☐	Red pen : Blue pen
Underline : Highlight	☐	Underline : Highlight
Spiral notebook : Three-ring binder	☐	Spiral notebook : Three-ring binder
Print : Cursive	☐	Print : Cursive
Front of class : Back of class	☐	Front of class : Back of class
Whiteboard : Chalkboard	☐	Whiteboard : Chalkboard
Shared table : Single desk	☐	Shared table : Single desk
Drive : Take the bus	☐	Drive : Take the bus
Backpack : Tote bag	☐	Backpack : Tote bag
A's and B's : C's and D's	☐	A's and B's : C's and D's
Tutor : Be tutored	☐	Tutor : Be tutored
Teacher's pet : Principal's office	☐	Teacher's pet : Principal's office

TOTAL MATCHED — ☐

Get to know each other better! Go to page 118.

FEARS

PLAYER 1	MARK **X** IF	PLAYER 2
Guess Player 2's answers	MATCHED ▼	Fill in your answers!

PLAYER 1			PLAYER 2	
Snakes	Spiders	☐	Snakes	Spiders
Heights	Depths	☐	Heights	Depths
Public speaking	Small talk	☐	Public speaking	Small talk
Flying	Driving	☐	Flying	Driving
Clowns	Dolls	☐	Clowns	Dolls
Darkness	Tight spaces	☐	Darkness	Tight spaces
Water	Fire	☐	Water	Fire
Rejection	Embarrassment	☐	Rejection	Embarrassment
Bugs	Rodents	☐	Bugs	Rodents
Crowds	Solitude	☐	Crowds	Solitude
Thunderstorms	Tornadoes	☐	Thunderstorms	Tornadoes
Blood	Needles	☐	Blood	Needles
Dentists	Doctors	☐	Dentists	Doctors
Ghosts	Aliens	☐	Ghosts	Aliens
Roller coasters	Haunted houses	☐	Roller coasters	Haunted houses
Germs	Dirt	☐	Germs	Dirt
Water slides	Bungee jumping	☐	Water slides	Bungee jumping
Public speaking	Public performance	☐	Public speaking	Public performance
Dogs	Cats	☐	Dogs	Cats
Holes	Outer space	☐	Holes	Outer space

TOTAL MATCHED — ☐

Get to know each other better! Go to page 118.

STORYBOOK ROLES

PLAYER 2 — Fill in your answers!		MARK **X** IF MATCHED ▼	PLAYER 1 — Guess Player 2's answers	
Captain	Pirate	☐	Captain	Pirate
Jedi	Sith	☐	Jedi	Sith
King	Queen	☐	King	Queen
Dumbledore	Voldemort	☐	Dumbledore	Voldemort
Genie	Fairy	☐	Genie	Fairy
Centaur	Mermaid	☐	Centaur	Mermaid
Batman	Superman	☐	Batman	Superman
Knight	Samurai	☐	Knight	Samurai
Secret agent	Adventurer	☐	Secret agent	Adventurer
Superhero	Villain	☐	Superhero	Villain
Time traveler	Intergalactic agent	☐	Time traveler	Intergalactic agent
Magician	Shape-shifter	☐	Magician	Shape-shifter
Hero	Sidekick	☐	Hero	Sidekick
Lion tamer	Horse whisperer	☐	Lion tamer	Horse whisperer
Bard	Jester	☐	Bard	Jester
Gladiator	Soldier	☐	Gladiator	Soldier
Goldsmith	Blacksmith	☐	Goldsmith	Blacksmith
Vampire	Werewolf	☐	Vampire	Werewolf
Cyborg	Robot	☐	Cyborg	Robot
Inventor	General	☐	Inventor	General

TOTAL MATCHED ⬚

Get to know each other better! Go to page 118.

CAREER IDEAS

PLAYER 1 — Guess Player 2's answers	MARK X IF MATCHED ▼	PLAYER 2 — Fill in your answers!
Coach : Athlete	☐	Coach : Athlete
Pop star : Rock star	☐	Pop star : Rock star
Chef : Waiter	☐	Chef : Waiter
Director : Producer	☐	Director : Producer
Detective : Spy	☐	Detective : Spy
President : Diplomat	☐	President : Diplomat
Talk show host : News anchor	☐	Talk show host : News anchor
Olympian : Sports announcer	☐	Olympian : Sports announcer
Mayor : Magician	☐	Mayor : Magician
Astronaut : Rocket scientist	☐	Astronaut : Rocket scientist
App creator : YouTuber	☐	App creator : YouTuber
Choreographer : Dancer	☐	Choreographer : Dancer
Author : Musician	☐	Author : Musician
Business owner : Artist	☐	Business owner : Artist
Firefighter : Policeman	☐	Firefighter : Policeman
Paleontologist : Geologist	☐	Paleontologist : Geologist
Doctor : Surgeon	☐	Doctor : Surgeon
Pilot : Lawyer	☐	Pilot : Lawyer
Veterinarian : Animal trainer	☐	Veterinarian : Animal trainer
Game designer : Fashion designer	☐	Game designer : Fashion designer

TOTAL MATCHED ☐

Get to know each other better! Go to page 118.

MY FUTURE

PLAYER 2 Fill in your answers!		MARK **X** IF MATCHED ▼	PLAYER 1 Guess Player 2's answers	
Higher education	Straight to work	☐	Higher education	Straight to work
Office job	Outdoor job	☐	Office job	Outdoor job
Big city	Small town	☐	Big city	Small town
Spender	Saver	☐	Spender	Saver
Travel abroad	Stay close to home	☐	Travel abroad	Stay close to home
Rent	Own	☐	Rent	Own
Pursue passion	Pursue stability	☐	Pursue passion	Pursue stability
Stay single	Get married	☐	Stay single	Get married
House	Apartment	☐	House	Apartment
Pets	No pets	☐	Pets	No pets
Children	No children	☐	Children	No children
Fame	Fortune	☐	Fame	Fortune
Live a long life	Live a happy life	☐	Live a long life	Live a happy life
Fancy car	Functional car	☐	Fancy car	Functional car
Community leader	Do your own thing	☐	Community leader	Do your own thing
Spend on home	Spend on experiences	☐	Spend on home	Spend on experiences
Buds with neighbors	Stays solitary	☐	Buds with neighbors	Stays solitary
Fulfillment	Financial success	☐	Fulfillment	Financial success
Stay up late	Wake up early	☐	Stay up late	Wake up early
Host parties	Attend parties	☐	Host parties	Attend parties

TOTAL MATCHED — ☐

Get to know each other better! Go to page 118.

CHAPTER 4

MEDIA

This chapter delves into everything from books, movies, and television to board games, video games, and art. Find out who loves competitive games or cooperative games, who prefers to laugh during a movie or cry during a movie, who picks up e-books or audiobooks, and more.

What do you gravitate toward?

ANYONE WHO HAS TIME
TO CLEAN IS CLEARLY NOT
READING ENOUGH.

BOOKS

PLAYER 1	MARK **X** IF	PLAYER 2
Guess Player 2's answers	MATCHED ▼	Fill in your answers!

Player 1		Match	Player 2	
Alice in Wonderland	The Wizard of Oz	☐	Alice in Wonderland	The Wizard of Oz
Classic	Contemporary	☐	Classic	Contemporary
Crime novels	Horror novels	☐	Crime novels	Horror novels
Diary of a Wimpy Kid	Big Nate	☐	Diary of a Wimpy Kid	Big Nate
Dracula	Frankenstein	☐	Dracula	Frankenstein
Fiction	Nonfiction	☐	Fiction	Nonfiction
Graphic novels	Traditional novels	☐	Graphic novels	Traditional novels
Hardcover	Paperback	☐	Hardcover	Paperback
Harry Potter	The Hunger Games	☐	Harry Potter	The Hunger Games
Lord of the Rings	Game of Thrones	☐	Lord of the Rings	Game of Thrones
Memoirs	Biographies	☐	Memoirs	Biographies
Physical books	E-books	☐	Physical books	E-books
Poetry	Short stories	☐	Poetry	Short stories
Bestseller	Critically acclaimed	☐	Bestseller	Critically acclaimed
Read before bed	Read in the morning	☐	Read before bed	Read in the morning
Read indoors	Read outdoors	☐	Read indoors	Read outdoors
Romance novels	Mystery novels	☐	Romance novels	Mystery novels
Science fiction	Fantasy	☐	Science fiction	Fantasy
Self-help books	Motivational books	☐	Self-help books	Motivational books
Series	Stand-alone novels	☐	Series	Stand-alone novels

TOTAL MATCHED ⸻ ☐

Get to know each other better! Go to page 119.

ART

<table>
<tr><td colspan="2">PLAYER 2
Fill in your answers!</td><td>MARK X IF
MATCHED
▼</td><td colspan="2">PLAYER 1
Guess Player 2's answers</td></tr>
<tr><td align="right">Paintings</td><td>Sculptures</td><td>☐</td><td align="right">Paintings</td><td>Sculptures</td></tr>
<tr><td align="right">Abstract</td><td>Realism</td><td>☐</td><td align="right">Abstract</td><td>Realism</td></tr>
<tr><td align="right">Watercolors</td><td>Oil paints</td><td>☐</td><td align="right">Watercolors</td><td>Oil paints</td></tr>
<tr><td align="right">Monochromatic</td><td>Colorful</td><td>☐</td><td align="right">Monochromatic</td><td>Colorful</td></tr>
<tr><td align="right">Landscape</td><td>Portrait</td><td>☐</td><td align="right">Landscape</td><td>Portrait</td></tr>
<tr><td align="right">Physical art</td><td>Digital art</td><td>☐</td><td align="right">Physical art</td><td>Digital art</td></tr>
<tr><td align="right">Interactive</td><td>Static</td><td>☐</td><td align="right">Interactive</td><td>Static</td></tr>
<tr><td align="right">Modern</td><td>Classical</td><td>☐</td><td align="right">Modern</td><td>Classical</td></tr>
<tr><td align="right">Acrylic</td><td>Charcoal</td><td>☐</td><td align="right">Acrylic</td><td>Charcoal</td></tr>
<tr><td align="right">Mixed media</td><td>Collage</td><td>☐</td><td align="right">Mixed media</td><td>Collage</td></tr>
<tr><td align="right">Street art</td><td>Gallery art</td><td>☐</td><td align="right">Street art</td><td>Gallery art</td></tr>
<tr><td align="right">Pencil</td><td>Pen</td><td>☐</td><td align="right">Pencil</td><td>Pen</td></tr>
<tr><td align="right">Graffiti</td><td>Murals</td><td>☐</td><td align="right">Graffiti</td><td>Murals</td></tr>
<tr><td align="right">Mosaics</td><td>Stained glass</td><td>☐</td><td align="right">Mosaics</td><td>Stained glass</td></tr>
<tr><td align="right">Pop art</td><td>Surrealism</td><td>☐</td><td align="right">Pop art</td><td>Surrealism</td></tr>
<tr><td align="right">Photography</td><td>Graphic design</td><td>☐</td><td align="right">Photography</td><td>Graphic design</td></tr>
<tr><td align="right">Art nouveau</td><td>Art deco</td><td>☐</td><td align="right">Art nouveau</td><td>Art deco</td></tr>
<tr><td align="right">Realistic</td><td>Impressionistic</td><td>☐</td><td align="right">Realistic</td><td>Impressionistic</td></tr>
<tr><td align="right">Western comics</td><td>Manga</td><td>☐</td><td align="right">Western comics</td><td>Manga</td></tr>
<tr><td align="right">Cool architecture</td><td>Cool packaging</td><td>☐</td><td align="right">Cool architecture</td><td>Cool packaging</td></tr>
</table>

TOTAL MATCHED ⬚

Get to know each other better! Go to page 119.

Get to know each other better! Go to page 119.

MOVIES & FILM

PLAYER 1		MARK **X** IF MATCHED ▼	PLAYER 2	
Guess Player 2's answers			Fill in your answers!	
Comedy	Horror	☐	Comedy	Horror
Horror	Thriller	☐	Horror	Thriller
Thriller	Drama	☐	Thriller	Drama
Drama	Comedy	☐	Drama	Comedy
Romance	Action	☐	Romance	Action
Science fiction	Western	☐	Science fiction	Western
Fantasy	Science fiction	☐	Fantasy	Science fiction
Documentary	True crime	☐	Documentary	True crime
A fun time	Makes you cry	☐	A fun time	Makes you cry
Animated	Live action	☐	Animated	Live action
Favorite actors	Favorite directors	☐	Favorite actors	Favorite directors
Musicals	Non-musicals	☐	Musicals	Non-musicals
Sequels	Originals	☐	Sequels	Originals
Blockbusters	Indies	☐	Blockbusters	Indies
Classic	Modern	☐	Classic	Modern
Popular	Niche	☐	Popular	Niche
Marvel	DC	☐	Marvel	DC
Star Wars	Star Trek	☐	Star Wars	Star Trek
Harry Potter	Lord of the Rings	☐	Harry Potter	Lord of the Rings
Disney	Pixar	☐	Disney	Pixar

TOTAL MATCHED ▭

Get to know each other better! Go to page 119.

MOVIE TIME

PLAYER 2 Fill in your answers!		MARK **X** IF MATCHED ▼	PLAYER 1 Guess Player 2's answers	
At home	In theater	☐	At home	In theater
3D	Regular	☐	3D	Regular
IMAX	Regular	☐	IMAX	Regular
Subtitles	No subtitles	☐	Subtitles	No subtitles
In the dark	With the lights on	☐	In the dark	With the lights on
Front-row seats	Back of the theater	☐	Front-row seats	Back of the theater
Near the aisle	Right in the middle	☐	Near the aisle	Right in the middle
Standard seats	Recliner seats	☐	Standard seats	Recliner seats
Stay for the credits	Leave at the end	☐	Stay for the credits	Leave at the end
Watch previews	Skip to the start	☐	Watch previews	Skip to the start
Old but cheap	New but expensive	☐	Old but cheap	New but expensive
Buttered popcorn	Kettle corn	☐	Buttered popcorn	Kettle corn
Slushie	Soda	☐	Slushie	Soda
Chocolate	Gummies	☐	Chocolate	Gummies
Popcorn	Candy	☐	Popcorn	Candy
Nachos	Hot dogs	☐	Nachos	Hot dogs
Water	Soda	☐	Water	Soda
Book first	Movie first	☐	Book first	Movie first
Oscars	Golden Globes	☐	Oscars	Golden Globes
3-hour film	2-hour film	☐	3-hour film	2-hour film

TOTAL MATCHED ⎯ ☐ **Get to know each other better! Go to page 119.**

SOCIAL MEDIA

PLAYER 1		MARK X IF	PLAYER 2	
PLAYER 1 Guess Player 2's answers		**MARK X IF MATCHED** ▼	**PLAYER 2** Fill in your answers!	
Instagram	TikTok	☐	Instagram	TikTok
Tumblr	Pinterest	☐	Tumblr	Pinterest
Twitter	Facebook	☐	Twitter	Facebook
Snapchat	YouTube	☐	Snapchat	YouTube
Stories	Posts	☐	Stories	Posts
Dog filter	Flower filter	☐	Dog filter	Flower filter
Beauty filters	Funny filters	☐	Beauty filters	Funny filters
Viral dances	Lip syncing	☐	Viral dances	Lip syncing
Vlogs	Hauls	☐	Vlogs	Hauls
Post with friends	Post alone	☐	Post with friends	Post alone
For you page	Explore page	☐	For you page	Explore page
High snap score	Low snap score	☐	High snap score	Low snap score
Likes	Comments	☐	Likes	Comments
Instagram stories	Snapchat stories	☐	Instagram stories	Snapchat stories
Black-and-white pics	Colored pics	☐	Black-and-white pics	Colored pics
Private story	Public story	☐	Private story	Public story
Messages	Facetime	☐	Messages	Facetime
Makeup tutorials	Hair tutorials	☐	Makeup tutorials	Hair tutorials
Recommended feed	Chronological feed	☐	Recommended feed	Chronological feed
Private account	Public account	☐	Private account	Public account

TOTAL MATCHED ☐

Get to know each other better! Go to page 119.

TELEVISION

PLAYER 2 — Fill in your answers!		MARK **X** IF MATCHED ▼	PLAYER 1 — Guess Player 2's answers	
Dramas	Comedies	☐	Dramas	Comedies
Live TV	Stream on demand	☐	Live TV	Stream on demand
Binge a series	Watch an episode	☐	Binge a series	Watch an episode
Watch alone	Watch with others	☐	Watch alone	Watch with others
TV in the morning	TV at night	☐	TV in the morning	TV at night
Local news	National news	☐	Local news	National news
Current shows	Classic shows	☐	Current shows	Classic shows
Reality	Scripted	☐	Reality	Scripted
Sports shows	Cooking shows	☐	Sports shows	Cooking shows
Watch on TV	Watch on computer	☐	Watch on TV	Watch on computer
Volume up	Subtitles on	☐	Volume up	Subtitles on
Sitcoms	Dramas	☐	Sitcoms	Dramas
Crime shows	Medical dramas	☐	Crime shows	Medical dramas
Animation	Live-action	☐	Animation	Live-action
Fantasy	Sci-fi	☐	Fantasy	Sci-fi
Happy ending	Sad ending	☐	Happy ending	Sad ending
Tons of action	Dialogue-heavy	☐	Tons of action	Dialogue-heavy
Set in the past	Set in the present	☐	Set in the past	Set in the present
Critically acclaimed	Guilty pleasure	☐	Critically acclaimed	Guilty pleasure
Ensemble cast	One big star	☐	Ensemble cast	One big star

TOTAL MATCHED ⬜

Get to know each other better! Go to page 119.

VIDEO GAMES

	PLAYER 1 Guess Player 2's answers	**MARK X IF MATCHED** ▼	**PLAYER 2** Fill in your answers!	

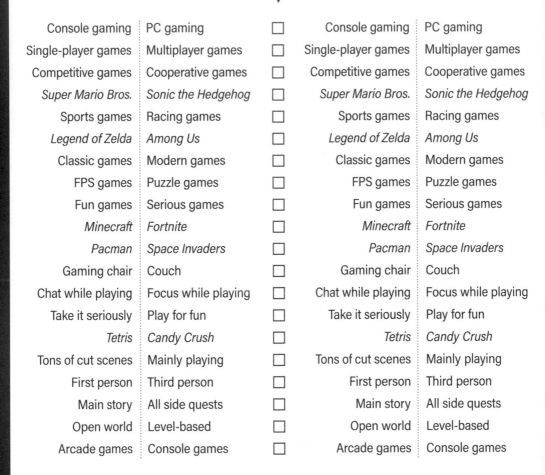

Console gaming	PC gaming	☐	Console gaming	PC gaming
Single-player games	Multiplayer games	☐	Single-player games	Multiplayer games
Competitive games	Cooperative games	☐	Competitive games	Cooperative games
Super Mario Bros.	*Sonic the Hedgehog*	☐	*Super Mario Bros.*	*Sonic the Hedgehog*
Sports games	Racing games	☐	Sports games	Racing games
Legend of Zelda	*Among Us*	☐	*Legend of Zelda*	*Among Us*
Classic games	Modern games	☐	Classic games	Modern games
FPS games	Puzzle games	☐	FPS games	Puzzle games
Fun games	Serious games	☐	Fun games	Serious games
Minecraft	*Fortnite*	☐	*Minecraft*	*Fortnite*
Pacman	*Space Invaders*	☐	*Pacman*	*Space Invaders*
Gaming chair	Couch	☐	Gaming chair	Couch
Chat while playing	Focus while playing	☐	Chat while playing	Focus while playing
Take it seriously	Play for fun	☐	Take it seriously	Play for fun
Tetris	*Candy Crush*	☐	*Tetris*	*Candy Crush*
Tons of cut scenes	Mainly playing	☐	Tons of cut scenes	Mainly playing
First person	Third person	☐	First person	Third person
Main story	All side quests	☐	Main story	All side quests
Open world	Level-based	☐	Open world	Level-based
Arcade games	Console games	☐	Arcade games	Console games

TOTAL MATCHED —

Get to know each other better! Go to page 119.

BOARD GAMES

PLAYER 2 Fill in your answers!		MARK X IF MATCHED	PLAYER 1 Guess Player 2's answers	
		▼		
Action games	Puzzle games	☐	Action games	Puzzle games
Battleship	Stratego	☐	Battleship	Stratego
Candy Land	Chutes and Ladders	☐	Candy Land	Chutes and Ladders
Chess	Checkers	☐	Chess	Checkers
Clue	Risk	☐	Clue	Risk
Competitive games	Cooperative games	☐	Competitive games	Cooperative games
Jenga	Twister	☐	Jenga	Twister
Monopoly	Scrabble	☐	Monopoly	Scrabble
Yahtzee	Boggle	☐	Yahtzee	Boggle
Multiplayer games	Single-player games	☐	Multiplayer games	Single-player games
Pictionary	Charades	☐	Pictionary	Charades
Strategy games	Chance games	☐	Strategy games	Chance games
Trading-card games	Collectible cards	☐	Trading-card games	Collectible cards
Trivia games	Word games	☐	Trivia games	Word games
Board games	Video games	☐	Board games	Video games
Board games	Lawn games	☐	Board games	Lawn games
Role-playing games	Card games	☐	Role-playing games	Card games
Poker	Uno	☐	Poker	Uno
Under an hour	Multiple hours	☐	Under an hour	Multiple hours
Simple rules	Tons of detail	☐	Simple rules	Tons of detail

TOTAL MATCHED ☐

Get to know each other better! Go to page 119.

CHAPTER 5

STYLE & FASHION

Style is subjective, but we've all got opinions on it! Go head to head in this chapter to find out which fashion accessories you reach for, you hair and grooming preferences, whether you like bright colors or neutral tones, and what shoes you always step out in.

Who's going to win this fashion show?

FASHION IS FICKLE,
BUT STYLE IS ALL YOU!

FASHION

PLAYER 1		MARK X IF MATCHED ▼	PLAYER 2	
Guess Player 2's answers			Fill in your answers!	
Bright colors	Neutral tones	☐	Bright colors	Neutral tones
High heels	Sneakers	☐	High heels	Sneakers
Skinny jeans	Wide-leg pants	☐	Skinny jeans	Wide-leg pants
Statement necklace	Delicate jewelry	☐	Statement necklace	Delicate jewelry
Leather jacket	Denim jacket	☐	Leather jacket	Denim jacket
Giant sunglasses	Aviators	☐	Giant sunglasses	Aviators
Fedora	Beanie	☐	Fedora	Beanie
Stripes	Polka dots	☐	Stripes	Polka dots
Lace	Leather	☐	Lace	Leather
Turtleneck	V-neck	☐	Turtleneck	V-neck
Beret	Baseball cap	☐	Beret	Baseball cap
High-waisted pants	Low-rise pants	☐	High-waisted pants	Low-rise pants
Sequins	Embroidery	☐	Sequins	Embroidery
Fanny pack	Crossbody bag	☐	Fanny pack	Crossbody bag
Flats	Boots	☐	Flats	Boots
Crop tops	Off-shoulder tops	☐	Crop tops	Off-shoulder tops
Long skirts	Short skirts	☐	Long skirts	Short skirts
Animal prints	Florals	☐	Animal prints	Florals
Velvet	Satin	☐	Velvet	Satin
Chokers	Long necklaces	☐	Chokers	Long necklaces

TOTAL MATCHED ⬚

Get to know each other better! Go to page 120.

SHOES

PLAYER 2		MARK X IF	PLAYER 1	
Fill in your answers!		MATCHED ▼	Guess Player 2's answers	
Heels	Flats	☐	Heels	Flats
Sandals	Flip-flops	☐	Sandals	Flip-flops
Hi-tops	Low tops	☐	Hi-tops	Low tops
High boots	Low boots	☐	High boots	Low boots
Stylish sneakers	Athletic sneakers	☐	Stylish sneakers	Athletic sneakers
Slippers	Crocs	☐	Slippers	Crocs
Wedges	Pumps	☐	Wedges	Pumps
Patterned shoes	Solid shoes	☐	Patterned shoes	Solid shoes
Black sneakers	White sneakers	☐	Black sneakers	White sneakers
Slip-ons	Lace-ups	☐	Slip-ons	Lace-ups
Rain boots	Snow boots	☐	Rain boots	Snow boots
Cowboy boots	Work boots	☐	Cowboy boots	Work boots
Leather shoes	Synthetic shoes	☐	Leather shoes	Synthetic shoes
Short heel	Tall heel	☐	Short heel	Tall heel
Platform sandals	Two-strap sandals	☐	Platform sandals	Two-strap sandals
Basketball sneakers	Cleats	☐	Basketball sneakers	Cleats
Pointy shoes	Round-toed shoes	☐	Pointy shoes	Round-toed shoes
Black boots	Brown boots	☐	Black boots	Brown boots
Gold heels	Silver heels	☐	Gold heels	Silver heels
Open-toe shoes	Closed-toe shoes	☐	Open-toe shoes	Closed-toe shoes

TOTAL MATCHED ⬚

Get to know each other better! Go to page 120.

ACCESSORIES

PLAYER 1		MARK X IF	PLAYER 2	
Guess Player 2's answers		**MATCHED** ▼	**Fill in your answers!**	
Necklaces	Bracelets	☐	Necklaces	Bracelets
Rings	Earrings	☐	Rings	Earrings
Tie	Bow tie	☐	Tie	Bow tie
Baseball cap	Bucket hat	☐	Baseball cap	Bucket hat
Belt	Chain	☐	Belt	Chain
Round glasses	Rectangle glasses	☐	Round glasses	Rectangle glasses
Cheap glasses	Designer glasses	☐	Cheap glasses	Designer glasses
Handbag	Clutch	☐	Handbag	Clutch
Purse	Tote bag	☐	Purse	Tote bag
Scarf	Beanie	☐	Scarf	Beanie
Black tights	Nude tights	☐	Black tights	Nude tights
Gloves	Mittens	☐	Gloves	Mittens
Headband	Bandana	☐	Headband	Bandana
Ankle socks	Crew socks	☐	Ankle socks	Crew socks
Solid socks	Printed socks	☐	Solid socks	Printed socks
Earmuffs	Winter hat	☐	Earmuffs	Winter hat
Cross-body bag	Shoulder bag	☐	Cross-body bag	Shoulder bag
Cute pin	Sassy pin	☐	Cute pin	Sassy pin
Color contacts	Lensless glasses	☐	Color contacts	Lensless glasses
Barrettes	Bobby pins	☐	Barrettes	Bobby pins

TOTAL MATCHED ____ ☐

Get to know each other better! Go to page 120.

HAIR

PLAYER 2 Fill in your answers!		MARK **X** IF MATCHED ▼	PLAYER 1 Guess Player 2's answers	
Long hair	Short hair	☐	Long hair	Short hair
Brown	Blonde	☐	Brown	Blonde
Straight	Curly	☐	Straight	Curly
Ponytail	Bun	☐	Ponytail	Bun
French braid	Classic braid	☐	French braid	Classic braid
High ponytail	Low ponytail	☐	High ponytail	Low ponytail
One braid	Two braids	☐	One braid	Two braids
Hair tie	Scrunchie	☐	Hair tie	Scrunchie
Middle part	Side part	☐	Middle part	Side part
Messy bun	Neat bun	☐	Messy bun	Neat bun
Bangs	No bangs	☐	Bangs	No bangs
Dyed hair	Natural hair	☐	Dyed hair	Natural hair
Loose curls	Tight curls	☐	Loose curls	Tight curls
Brush	Comb	☐	Brush	Comb
Hairspray	Hair gel	☐	Hairspray	Hair gel
Curling iron	Curling wand	☐	Curling iron	Curling wand
Blow-dry	Air-dry	☐	Blow-dry	Air-dry
Ribbon	Hair bow	☐	Ribbon	Hair bow
Half up, half down	Fancy updo	☐	Half up, half down	Fancy updo
Claw clip	Barrette	☐	Claw clip	Barrette

TOTAL MATCHED — ☐

Get to know each other better! Go to page 120.

MAKEUP

PLAYER 1		MARK **X** IF MATCHED ▼	PLAYER 2	
Guess Player 2's answers			Fill in your answers!	
Natural look	Full glam	☐	Natural look	Full glam
Winged eyeliner	Regular eyeliner	☐	Winged eyeliner	Regular eyeliner
Bold lip	Nude lip	☐	Bold lip	Nude lip
Lipstick	Lip gloss	☐	Lipstick	Lip gloss
Glitter eyeshadow	Solid eyeshadow	☐	Glitter eyeshadow	Solid eyeshadow
Lengthening mascara	Volume mascara	☐	Lengthening mascara	Volume mascara
Beauty blender	Makeup brush	☐	Beauty blender	Makeup brush
Drugstore makeup	High-end makeup	☐	Drugstore makeup	High-end makeup
Cream blush	Powder blush	☐	Cream blush	Powder blush
Colored eye shadow	Neutral eye shadow	☐	Colored eye shadow	Neutral eye shadow
Liquid concealer	Stick concealer	☐	Liquid concealer	Stick concealer
Highlighter	Bronzer	☐	Highlighter	Bronzer
Liquid eyeliner	Pencil eyeliner	☐	Liquid eyeliner	Pencil eyeliner
Smoky eye	Subtle eye	☐	Smoky eye	Subtle eye
Tinted lip balm	Regular lip balm	☐	Tinted lip balm	Regular lip balm
Brown mascara	Black mascara	☐	Brown mascara	Black mascara
Matte lips	Glossy lips	☐	Matte lips	Glossy lips
Straight eyebrows	Arched eyebrows	☐	Straight eyebrows	Arched eyebrows
Thick eyebrows	Thin eyebrows	☐	Thick eyebrows	Thin eyebrows
Foundation	Natural	☐	Foundation	Natural

TOTAL MATCHED ⏵ ☐

Get to know each other better! Go to page 120.

GROOMING

<table>
<tr><th colspan="2">PLAYER 2
Fill in your answers!</th><th>MARK X IF
MATCHED
▼</th><th colspan="2">PLAYER 1
Guess Player 2's answers</th></tr>
<tr><td>Showers</td><td>Baths</td><td>☐</td><td>Showers</td><td>Baths</td></tr>
<tr><td>Bar soap</td><td>Liquid soap</td><td>☐</td><td>Bar soap</td><td>Liquid soap</td></tr>
<tr><td>Shampoo only</td><td>Add conditioner</td><td>☐</td><td>Shampoo only</td><td>Add conditioner</td></tr>
<tr><td>Clean shave</td><td>Facial hair</td><td>☐</td><td>Clean shave</td><td>Facial hair</td></tr>
<tr><td>Tweezing</td><td>Waxing</td><td>☐</td><td>Tweezing</td><td>Waxing</td></tr>
<tr><td>Nail clippers</td><td>Nail file</td><td>☐</td><td>Nail clippers</td><td>Nail file</td></tr>
<tr><td>Nail polish</td><td>Naked nails</td><td>☐</td><td>Nail polish</td><td>Naked nails</td></tr>
<tr><td>Lip balm</td><td>Lipstick</td><td>☐</td><td>Lip balm</td><td>Lipstick</td></tr>
<tr><td>Perfume</td><td>Body spray</td><td>☐</td><td>Perfume</td><td>Body spray</td></tr>
<tr><td>Hairbrush</td><td>Comb</td><td>☐</td><td>Hairbrush</td><td>Comb</td></tr>
<tr><td>Hair gel</td><td>Hairspray</td><td>☐</td><td>Hair gel</td><td>Hairspray</td></tr>
<tr><td>Natural hair</td><td>Highlights</td><td>☐</td><td>Natural hair</td><td>Highlights</td></tr>
<tr><td>Teeth whitening</td><td>Natural teeth</td><td>☐</td><td>Teeth whitening</td><td>Natural teeth</td></tr>
<tr><td>Flossing teeth</td><td>Brushing teeth only</td><td>☐</td><td>Flossing teeth</td><td>Brushing teeth only</td></tr>
<tr><td>Makeup</td><td>No makeup</td><td>☐</td><td>Makeup</td><td>No makeup</td></tr>
<tr><td>Hair extensions</td><td>Natural hair length</td><td>☐</td><td>Hair extensions</td><td>Natural hair length</td></tr>
<tr><td>Regular hair trims</td><td>Let the hair grow</td><td>☐</td><td>Regular hair trims</td><td>Let the hair grow</td></tr>
<tr><td>Morning showers</td><td>Night showers</td><td>☐</td><td>Morning showers</td><td>Night showers</td></tr>
<tr><td>Curling iron</td><td>Straightener</td><td>☐</td><td>Curling iron</td><td>Straightener</td></tr>
<tr><td>Bronzer</td><td>Highlight</td><td>☐</td><td>Bronzer</td><td>Highlight</td></tr>
</table>

**TOTAL
MATCHED**

Get to know each other better! Go to page 120.

JEWELRY

PLAYER 1 Guess Player 2's answers	MARK X IF MATCHED ▼	PLAYER 2 Fill in your answers!
Gold : Silver	☐	Gold : Silver
Copper : Bronze	☐	Copper : Bronze
Wood : Shell	☐	Wood : Shell
Earrings : Necklace	☐	Earrings : Necklace
Bracelet : Anklet	☐	Bracelet : Anklet
Statement : Dainty	☐	Statement : Dainty
Hoops : Studs	☐	Hoops : Studs
Diamond : Pearl	☐	Diamond : Pearl
Pendant : Choker	☐	Pendant : Choker
Long : Short	☐	Long : Short
Stackable : Single	☐	Stackable : Single
Chain : Cord	☐	Chain : Cord
Locket : Charm bracelet	☐	Locket : Charm bracelet
Bold : Subtle	☐	Bold : Subtle
Cuff : Bangle	☐	Cuff : Bangle
Rhinestones : Turquoise	☐	Rhinestones : Turquoise
Classic : Modern	☐	Classic : Modern
New : Vintage	☐	New : Vintage
DIY : Store-bought	☐	DIY : Store-bought
Costume : Fine	☐	Costume : Fine

TOTAL MATCHED ⎯ ☐

Get to know each other better! Go to page 120.

BODY MODS

PLAYER 2 Fill in your answers!		MARK X IF MATCHED ▼	PLAYER 1 Guess Player 2's answers	
One piercing	Many piercings	☐	One piercing	Many piercings
Septum piercing	Nostril piercing	☐	Septum piercing	Nostril piercing
Nose piercing	Eyebrow piercing	☐	Nose piercing	Eyebrow piercing
Tongue piercing	Lip piercing	☐	Tongue piercing	Lip piercing
Ear piercing	Dermal piercing	☐	Ear piercing	Dermal piercing
Lobe piercing	Helix piercing	☐	Lobe piercing	Helix piercing
Conch piercing	Tragus piercing	☐	Conch piercing	Tragus piercing
One tattoo	Many tattoos	☐	One tattoo	Many tattoos
Black tattoos	Color tattoos	☐	Black tattoos	Color tattoos
Line tattoos	Shaded tattoos	☐	Line tattoos	Shaded tattoos
Realistic tattoos	Artistic tattoos	☐	Realistic tattoos	Artistic tattoos
Tattoo sleeve	Scattered tattoos	☐	Tattoo sleeve	Scattered tattoos
Machine tattoos	Stick and poke	☐	Machine tattoos	Stick and poke
Meaningful tattoos	Just for the art	☐	Meaningful tattoos	Just for the art
Plastic surgery	Keep it natural	☐	Plastic surgery	Keep it natural
Lip filler	Botox	☐	Lip filler	Botox
Nose job	Tummy tuck	☐	Nose job	Tummy tuck
Liposuction	Facelift	☐	Liposuction	Facelift
Hair transplant	Tattooed makeup	☐	Hair transplant	Tattooed makeup
Dermabrasion	Laser hair removal	☐	Dermabrasion	Laser hair removal

TOTAL MATCHED ☐

Get to know each other better! Go to page 120.

CHAPTER 6

THE WORLD

Whether you're a true homebody or an aspiring jetsetter, there are tons of questions here for you. Find out who prefers the beach or the mountains, who wants to hit up Ireland or Iceland, who packs light or brings their whole closet, and more.

Adventure (and knowledge) await.

I HAVEN'T BEEN
EVERYWHERE YET,
BUT IT'S ON MY LIST.

DESTINATION CITIES

		MARK **X** IF MATCHED ▼		
PLAYER 1 Guess Player 2's answers			**PLAYER 2** Fill in your answers!	
Paris	Rome	☐	Paris	Rome
New York	New Orleans	☐	New York	New Orleans
London	Los Angeles	☐	London	Los Angeles
Beijing	Berlin	☐	Beijing	Berlin
Sydney	Seattle	☐	Sydney	Seattle
San Francisco	St. Tropez	☐	San Francisco	St. Tropez
Dubai	Dublin	☐	Dubai	Dublin
Honolulu	Madrid	☐	Honolulu	Madrid
Barcelona	Tokyo	☐	Barcelona	Tokyo
Hong Kong	Amsterdam	☐	Hong Kong	Amsterdam
Miami	Montreal	☐	Miami	Montreal
Las Vegas	Nashville	☐	Las Vegas	Nashville
San Diego	San Juan	☐	San Diego	San Juan
Cape Town	Cairo	☐	Cape Town	Cairo
Mumbai	Sydney	☐	Mumbai	Sydney
Boston	Chicago	☐	Boston	Chicago
Havana	Rio de Janeiro	☐	Havana	Rio de Janeiro
Bangkok	Seoul	☐	Bangkok	Seoul
Moscow	Milan	☐	Moscow	Milan
Anchorage	Athens	☐	Anchorage	Athens

TOTAL MATCHED ☐

Get to know each other better! Go to page 121.

SIGHTS TO SEE

PLAYER 2
Fill in your answers!

MARK X IF MATCHED
▼

PLAYER 1
Guess Player 2's answers

Player 2		Matched	Player 1	
Disney World	Universal Studios	☐	Disney World	Universal Studios
Hawaii	Alaska	☐	Hawaii	Alaska
Yellowstone	Yosemite	☐	Yellowstone	Yosemite
Hollywood	Times Square	☐	Hollywood	Times Square
Grand Canyon	Mount Rushmore	☐	Grand Canyon	Mount Rushmore
Brooklyn Bridge	Golden Gate Bridge	☐	Brooklyn Bridge	Golden Gate Bridge
Disneyland	Legoland	☐	Disneyland	Legoland
San Diego Zoo	Bronx Zoo	☐	San Diego Zoo	Bronx Zoo
Kennedy Space Center	Smithsonian	☐	Kennedy Space Center	Smithsonian
Niagara Falls	The Florida Keys	☐	Niagara Falls	The Florida Keys
Sydney Opera House	Kangaroo Island	☐	Sydney Opera House	Kangaroo Island
Blue Ridge Mountains	Rocky Mountains	☐	Blue Ridge Mountains	Rocky Mountains
Lake Michigan	Lake Tahoe	☐	Lake Michigan	Lake Tahoe
Yankee Stadium	Fenway Park	☐	Yankee Stadium	Fenway Park
White House	Graceland	☐	White House	Graceland
Death Valley	Joshua Tree	☐	Death Valley	Joshua Tree
Great Barrier Reef	Uluru	☐	Great Barrier Reef	Uluru
Monument Valley	A redwood forest	☐	Monument Valley	A redwood forest
The Bean	Wrigley Field	☐	The Bean	Wrigley Field
Northern Lights	South Pole	☐	Northern Lights	South Pole

TOTAL MATCHED ☐

Get to know each other better! Go to page 121.

COUNTRIES TO VISIT

PLAYER 1		MARK X IF MATCHED ▼	PLAYER 2	
PLAYER 1 Guess Player 2's answers			**PLAYER 2** Fill in your answers!	
Norway	Sweden	☐	Norway	Sweden
Brazil	Portugal	☐	Brazil	Portugal
South Korea	Japan	☐	South Korea	Japan
Vietnam	Thailand	☐	Vietnam	Thailand
Morocco	Egypt	☐	Morocco	Egypt
New Zealand	Australia	☐	New Zealand	Australia
The Bahamas	Costa Rica	☐	The Bahamas	Costa Rica
Germany	Italy	☐	Germany	Italy
Argentina	Peru	☐	Argentina	Peru
United Kingdom	Canada	☐	United Kingdom	Canada
France	Greece	☐	France	Greece
Ethiopia	Kenya	☐	Ethiopia	Kenya
Turkey	Israel	☐	Turkey	Israel
China	Indonesia	☐	China	Indonesia
Malaysia	Singapore	☐	Malaysia	Singapore
South Africa	Madagascar	☐	South Africa	Madagascar
Ireland	Iceland	☐	Ireland	Iceland
India	Nepal	☐	India	Nepal
Mexico	Spain	☐	Mexico	Spain
Switzerland	The Netherlands	☐	Switzerland	The Netherlands

TOTAL MATCHED — ☐

Get to know each other better! Go to page 121.

INTERNATIONAL CUISINE

PLAYER 2 — Fill in your answers!		MARK **X** IF MATCHED ▼	PLAYER 1 — Guess Player 2's answers	
Sushi	Pizza	☐	Sushi	Pizza
Tacos	Pad thai	☐	Tacos	Pad thai
Falafel	Gyro	☐	Falafel	Gyro
Croissant	Bagel	☐	Croissant	Bagel
Ramen	Pho	☐	Ramen	Pho
Curry	Tandoori	☐	Curry	Tandoori
Empanada	Samosa	☐	Empanada	Samosa
Hummus	Guacamole	☐	Hummus	Guacamole
Kimchi	Sauerkraut	☐	Kimchi	Sauerkraut
Paella	Risotto	☐	Paella	Risotto
Dumplings	Pierogies	☐	Dumplings	Pierogies
Kebab	Shawarma	☐	Kebab	Shawarma
Crepe	Waffle	☐	Crepe	Waffle
Borscht	Gazpacho	☐	Borscht	Gazpacho
Couscous	Quinoa	☐	Couscous	Quinoa
Pesto	Chimichurri	☐	Pesto	Chimichurri
Jerk	Curry	☐	Jerk	Curry
Goulash	Schnitzel	☐	Goulash	Schnitzel
Gumbo	Jambalaya	☐	Gumbo	Jambalaya
Gelato	Mochi	☐	Gelato	Mochi

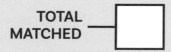

TOTAL MATCHED — ☐   **Get to know each other better! Go to page 121.**

ENVIRONMENT

PLAYER 1		MARK **X** IF MATCHED ▼		PLAYER 2	
PLAYER 1 Guess Player 2's answers				**PLAYER 2** Fill in your answers!	
Recycling	Throwing away	☐		Recycling	Throwing away
Walking	Driving	☐		Walking	Driving
Lots of lights	Limited lights	☐		Lots of lights	Limited lights
Ignoring litter	Picking up litter	☐		Ignoring litter	Picking up litter
Faucet running	Faucet off	☐		Faucet running	Faucet off
Cloth napkins	Paper napkins	☐		Cloth napkins	Paper napkins
Reusable cup	Disposable cup	☐		Reusable cup	Disposable cup
Bottled water	Tap water	☐		Bottled water	Tap water
Gadgets plugged in	Gadgets unplugged	☐		Gadgets plugged in	Gadgets unplugged
Planting trees	Planting flowers	☐		Planting trees	Planting flowers
Eating vegetables	Eating meat	☐		Eating vegetables	Eating meat
Short showers	Long baths	☐		Short showers	Long baths
Playing outside	Watching TV	☐		Playing outside	Watching TV
Reusable lunchbox	Brown paper bag	☐		Reusable lunchbox	Brown paper bag
Plastic straw	No straw	☐		Plastic straw	No straw
Thrifting	Buying new	☐		Thrifting	Buying new
Local store	Big-box store	☐		Local store	Big-box store
Repairing	Replacing	☐		Repairing	Replacing
AC on	Windows open	☐		AC on	Windows open
Flying	Taking the train	☐		Flying	Taking the train

TOTAL MATCHED — ☐

Get to know each other better! Go to page 121.

NATURE

| PLAYER 2 | MARK **X** IF | PLAYER 1 |
| Fill in your answers! | MATCHED ▼ | Guess Player 2's answers |

Player 2		Matched	Player 1	
Butterflies	Birds	☐	Butterflies	Birds
Flowers	Trees	☐	Flowers	Trees
Ocean	Mountains	☐	Ocean	Mountains
Sun	Moon	☐	Sun	Moon
Water	Snow	☐	Water	Snow
Forest	Meadow	☐	Forest	Meadow
Wildflowers	Seagrass	☐	Wildflowers	Seagrass
Clouds	Stars	☐	Clouds	Stars
Stars	Rainbows	☐	Stars	Rainbows
Dirt	Sand	☐	Dirt	Sand
Bugs	Snakes	☐	Bugs	Snakes
Songbirds	Hawks	☐	Songbirds	Hawks
Sea	River	☐	Sea	River
Canyon	Valley	☐	Canyon	Valley
Forest	Jungle	☐	Forest	Jungle
Bees	Flies	☐	Bees	Flies
Snow	Ice	☐	Snow	Ice
Seashells	Rocks	☐	Seashells	Rocks
Park	Pasture	☐	Park	Pasture
Moths	Dragonflies	☐	Moths	Dragonflies

TOTAL MATCHED — ☐

Get to know each other better! Go to page 121.

WEATHER

PLAYER 1 Guess Player 2's answers	MARK **X** IF MATCHED ▼	PLAYER 2 Fill in your answers!
Sunny day : Rainy day	☐	Sunny day : Rainy day
Sun shower : Snow flurries	☐	Sun shower : Snow flurries
Heavy winds : Heavy rain	☐	Heavy winds : Heavy rain
Raincoat : Umbrella	☐	Raincoat : Umbrella
Thunder : Lightning	☐	Thunder : Lightning
Fog : Sleet	☐	Fog : Sleet
Rainy morning : Rainy afternoon	☐	Rainy morning : Rainy afternoon
Heat wave : Below freezing	☐	Heat wave : Below freezing
Blizzard : Hurricane	☐	Blizzard : Hurricane
Tornado : Earthquake	☐	Tornado : Earthquake
Rain boots : Snow boots	☐	Rain boots : Snow boots
Flood : Drought	☐	Flood : Drought
Sunburn : Windburn	☐	Sunburn : Windburn
Chilly : Warm	☐	Chilly : Warm
Puddle jumping : Sledding	☐	Puddle jumping : Sledding
High tide : Low tide	☐	High tide : Low tide
Sunrise : Sunset	☐	Sunrise : Sunset
Heatstroke : Frostbite	☐	Heatstroke : Frostbite
Hailstorm : Dust storm	☐	Hailstorm : Dust storm
Online forecast : Local TV forecast	☐	Online forecast : Local TV forecast

TOTAL MATCHED ☐

Get to know each other better! Go to page 121.

VACATION

PLAYER 2 — Fill in your answers!		MARK X IF MATCHED ▼	PLAYER 1 — Guess Player 2's answers	
Beach	Mountains	☐	Beach	Mountains
Road trip	Flight	☐	Road trip	Flight
Camping	Glamping	☐	Camping	Glamping
Pool	Ocean	☐	Pool	Ocean
Sightseeing	Relaxing	☐	Sightseeing	Relaxing
Big city	Small town	☐	Big city	Small town
Tropical island	Snowy resort	☐	Tropical island	Snowy resort
Fancy hotel	Cool rental	☐	Fancy hotel	Cool rental
National parks	Hidden gems	☐	National parks	Hidden gems
Group vacation	Solo travel	☐	Group vacation	Solo travel
Domestic	Foreign	☐	Domestic	Foreign
RV	Tent	☐	RV	Tent
Laid back	Luxury	☐	Laid back	Luxury
Travel with friends	Travel with family	☐	Travel with friends	Travel with family
Pack light	Bring everything	☐	Pack light	Bring everything
Tour guide	Self-guided	☐	Tour guide	Self-guided
Planned	Spontaneous	☐	Planned	Spontaneous
Late for flight	Early for flight	☐	Late for flight	Early for flight
Lakefront	Oceanfront	☐	Lakefront	Oceanfront
Dress your best	Dress super casual	☐	Dress your best	Dress super casual

TOTAL MATCHED ⎯ ☐

Get to know each other better! Go to page 121.

CHAPTER 7

FUN STUFF

This chapter is dedicated to the fun stuff in life, and it's guaranteed to get you laughing with your fellow players. You'll learn how you like to spend your holidays, who everyone's favorite superheroes are, where you'd travel in time, and—importantly— whether you boogie down to the Macarena or the Electric Slide!

Let's dive in!

HAVING FUN IS LIKE
SPRINKLING CONFETTI
ON YOUR WORRIES.

HOLIDAYS

PLAYER 1		MARK X IF	PLAYER 2	
Guess Player 2's answers		MATCHED ▼	Fill in your answers!	
Big gatherings	Small get-togethers	☐	Big gatherings	Small get-togethers
Dressy	Casual	☐	Dressy	Casual
Homemade décor	Store-bought décor	☐	Homemade décor	Store-bought décor
Cook at home	Order in	☐	Cook at home	Order in
Parades	Fireworks	☐	Parades	Fireworks
Live music	Live show	☐	Live music	Live show
Stay home	Visit family	☐	Stay home	Visit family
Barbecue	Fancy dinner	☐	Barbecue	Fancy dinner
Religious service	Family walk	☐	Religious service	Family walk
One master chef	Potluck	☐	One master chef	Potluck
Host at home	Event venue	☐	Host at home	Event venue
Cozy in winter	Outdoor in summer	☐	Cozy in winter	Outdoor in summer
Day off during week	Long weekend	☐	Day off during week	Long weekend
Friends and family	Just family	☐	Friends and family	Just family
Adults only	Adults and kids	☐	Adults only	Adults and kids
Holiday movies	Holiday songs	☐	Holiday movies	Holiday songs
Age-old traditions	New traditions	☐	Age-old traditions	New traditions
Multiday affair	Just one day	☐	Multiday affair	Just one day
Raucous and lively	Quiet and thoughtful	☐	Raucous and lively	Quiet and thoughtful
Celebrate alone	Celebrate with others	☐	Celebrate alone	Celebrate with others

TOTAL MATCHED ____ ☐

Get to know each other better! Go to page 122.

CARS

	PLAYER 2 Fill in your answers!	MARK **X** IF MATCHED ▼		PLAYER 1 Guess Player 2's answers
Back road	Highway	☐	Back road	Highway
Car radio	Your playlist	☐	Car radio	Your playlist
Carpool	Solo driving	☐	Carpool	Solo driving
Carpool karaoke	Carpool silence	☐	Carpool karaoke	Carpool silence
Classic muscle car	Sleek sports car	☐	Classic muscle car	Sleek sports car
Fast car	Fuel-efficient car	☐	Fast car	Fuel-efficient car
Heated seats	Sunroof	☐	Heated seats	Sunroof
Leather seats	Killer sound system	☐	Leather seats	Killer sound system
Luxury car	Economy car	☐	Luxury car	Economy car
Big SUV	Little sedan	☐	Big SUV	Little sedan
Vanity plate	Standard plate	☐	Vanity plate	Standard plate
Red car	Black car	☐	Red car	Black car
Road rage	Calm and collected	☐	Road rage	Calm and collected
Stick with one car	Change cars a lot	☐	Stick with one car	Change cars a lot
Music	Podcast	☐	Music	Podcast
Vintage car	Modern car	☐	Vintage car	Modern car
Window tinting	No tinting	☐	Window tinting	No tinting
Windows open	AC on	☐	Windows open	AC on
Beep the horn	Smile and wave	☐	Beep the horn	Smile and wave
Park close	Park far away	☐	Park close	Park far away

TOTAL MATCHED ☐

Get to know each other better! Go to page 122.

GAME SHOWS

PLAYER 1		MARK X IF MATCHED ▼	PLAYER 2	
Guess Player 2's answers			**Fill in your answers!**	
Host	Contestant	☐	Host	Contestant
Win money	Win prizes	☐	Win money	Win prizes
Trivia	Physical challenges	☐	Trivia	Physical challenges
Play alone	Play on a team	☐	Play alone	Play on a team
Fast-paced	Slow-paced	☐	Fast-paced	Slow-paced
Solo host	Multiple hosts	☐	Solo host	Multiple hosts
Kind host	Sarcastic host	☐	Kind host	Sarcastic host
Knowledge	Skill	☐	Knowledge	Skill
Based on luck	Based on skill	☐	Based on luck	Based on skill
Live audience	No audience	☐	Live audience	No audience
High-pressure	Relaxed	☐	High-pressure	Relaxed
Celebrities	Regular people	☐	Celebrities	Regular people
Silly	Serious	☐	Silly	Serious
Television	Streaming	☐	Television	Streaming
Retro	Current	☐	Retro	Current
Filmed	Live	☐	Filmed	Live
Aggressive game	Chill game	☐	Aggressive game	Chill game
Phone a friend	Ask the audience	☐	Phone a friend	Ask the audience
Jeopardy!	*Wheel of Fortune*	☐	*Jeopardy!*	*Wheel of Fortune*
Family Feud	*The Price Is Right*	☐	*Family Feud*	*The Price Is Right*

TOTAL MATCHED ☐

Get to know each other better! Go to page 122.

FLOWERS

PLAYER 2 Fill in your answers!		MARK **X** IF MATCHED ▼	PLAYER 1 Guess Player 2's answers	
Rose	Tulip	☐	Rose	Tulip
Sunflower	Daisy	☐	Sunflower	Daisy
Lily	Orchid	☐	Lily	Orchid
Peony	Hydrangea	☐	Peony	Hydrangea
Marigold	Gardenia	☐	Marigold	Gardenia
Chrysanthemum	Carnation	☐	Chrysanthemum	Carnation
Petunia	Pansy	☐	Petunia	Pansy
Cherry blossom	Sweet pea	☐	Cherry blossom	Sweet pea
Dandelion	Lavender	☐	Dandelion	Lavender
Geranium	Lotus	☐	Geranium	Lotus
Jasmine	Hibiscus	☐	Jasmine	Hibiscus
Daffodil	Dahlia	☐	Daffodil	Dahlia
Poppy	Snowdrop	☐	Poppy	Snowdrop
Lilac	Poinsettia	☐	Lilac	Poinsettia
Iris	Snapdragon	☐	Iris	Snapdragon
Red rose	Pink rose	☐	Red rose	Pink rose
Mixed bouquet	Single bouquet	☐	Mixed bouquet	Single bouquet
Corsage	Bouquet	☐	Corsage	Bouquet
Grocery store	Florist	☐	Grocery store	Florist
Fresh flowers	Dried flowers	☐	Fresh flowers	Dried flowers

TOTAL MATCHED ☐

Get to know each other better! Go to page 122.

DANCE MOVES

	PLAYER 1	MARK X IF	PLAYER 2	
	Guess Player 2's answers	MATCHED ▼	Fill in your answers!	

PLAYER 1		MARK X IF MATCHED	PLAYER 2	
Moonwalk	The Running Man	☐	Moonwalk	The Running Man
Twerking	The Robot	☐	Twerking	The Robot
Slow dancing	Fast dancing	☐	Slow dancing	Fast dancing
Flossing	The Electric Slide	☐	Flossing	The Electric Slide
Breakdancing	Tango	☐	Breakdancing	Tango
The Dougie	The Twist	☐	The Dougie	The Twist
The Macarena	The Cha Cha Slide	☐	The Macarena	The Cha Cha Slide
Salsa	Swing	☐	Salsa	Swing
Ballet	Jazz	☐	Ballet	Jazz
With a partner	In a group	☐	With a partner	In a group
Tap	Hip-hop	☐	Tap	Hip-hop
Ballroom	Contemporary	☐	Ballroom	Contemporary
Belly dancing	Flamenco	☐	Belly dancing	Flamenco
Bollywood	YMCA	☐	Bollywood	YMCA
House	Techno	☐	House	Techno
Irish step dance	Clogging	☐	Irish step dance	Clogging
Disco dancing	Line dancing	☐	Disco dancing	Line dancing
Live band	DJ	☐	Live band	DJ
First to dance	Last to dance	☐	First to dance	Last to dance
Choreography	Improv	☐	Choreography	Improv

TOTAL MATCHED — ☐

Get to know each other better! Go to page 122.

SUPERHEROES

PLAYER 2 — Fill in your answers!		MARK X IF MATCHED ▼	PLAYER 1 — Guess Player 2's answers	
Spidey-sense	Super strength	☐	Spidey-sense	Super strength
Batman	Superman	☐	Batman	Superman
Telekinesis	Invisibility	☐	Telekinesis	Invisibility
Mask	No mask	☐	Mask	No mask
Mind control	Teleportation	☐	Mind control	Teleportation
Wonder Woman	Captain Marvel	☐	Wonder Woman	Captain Marvel
Shapeshifting	Super hearing	☐	Shapeshifting	Super hearing
X-ray vision	Laser vision	☐	X-ray vision	Laser vision
Hulk	Thor	☐	Hulk	Thor
Black Panther	Wolverine	☐	Black Panther	Wolverine
Super speed	Precognition	☐	Super speed	Precognition
Time travel	Flight	☐	Time travel	Flight
Power of illusion	Perfect luck	☐	Power of illusion	Perfect luck
Peter Parker	Clark Kent	☐	Peter Parker	Clark Kent
Healing powers	Force fields	☐	Healing powers	Force fields
Shield	Cape	☐	Shield	Cape
Catwoman	Robin	☐	Catwoman	Robin
Mind reading	Elasticity	☐	Mind reading	Elasticity
Utility belt	Tricked-out car	☐	Utility belt	Tricked-out car
Faithful sidekick	Flying solo	☐	Faithful sidekick	Flying solo

TOTAL MATCHED ☐

Get to know each other better! Go to page 122.

TIME TRAVEL

PLAYER 1	MARK **X** IF	PLAYER 2
Guess Player 2's answers	MATCHED ▼	Fill in your answers!

Ancestors	Future self	☐	Ancestors	Future self
Steve Jobs	Thomas Edison	☐	Steve Jobs	Thomas Edison
Walt Disney	Dr. Seuss	☐	Walt Disney	Dr. Seuss
Woodstock	Beatles concert	☐	Woodstock	Beatles concert
Moon landing	Mars landing	☐	Moon landing	Mars landing
Past president	First lady president	☐	Past president	First lady president
Classic cars	Electric cars	☐	Classic cars	Electric cars
Ancient Rome	Ancient Egypt	☐	Ancient Rome	Ancient Egypt
Dark Ages	Renaissance	☐	Dark Ages	Renaissance
Roaring Twenties	1950s	☐	Roaring Twenties	1950s
Ancient China	Ancient Japan	☐	Ancient China	Ancient Japan
Explorer's ship	Robin Hood's forest	☐	Explorer's ship	Robin Hood's forest
Wild West	Shakespeare's time	☐	Wild West	Shakespeare's time
1960s	2060s	☐	1960s	2060s
Regency period	King Arthur's court	☐	Regency period	King Arthur's court
Neanderthal times	Dinosaur age	☐	Neanderthal times	Dinosaur age
The year 1000	The year 3000	☐	The year 1000	The year 3000
Lewis & Clark	Darwin's voyage	☐	Lewis & Clark	Darwin's voyage
Stone Age	Viking Age	☐	Stone Age	Viking Age
Victorian era	Edwardian era	☐	Victorian era	Edwardian era

TOTAL MATCHED ☐

Get to know each other better! Go to page 122.

SUPERSTITIONS & LUCK

PLAYER 2 Fill in your answers!		MARK **X** IF MATCHED ▼	PLAYER 1 Guess Player 2's answers	
Black cat	Broken mirror	☐	Black cat	Broken mirror
Four-leaf clover	Horseshoe	☐	Four-leaf clover	Horseshoe
Step on crack	Walk under ladder	☐	Step on crack	Walk under ladder
Knock on wood	Cross fingers	☐	Knock on wood	Cross fingers
Rabbit's foot	Lucky coin	☐	Rabbit's foot	Lucky coin
Friday the 13th	Full moon	☐	Friday the 13th	Full moon
Salt over shoulder	Blow on dandelion	☐	Salt over shoulder	Blow on dandelion
Open umbrella inside	Whistle inside	☐	Open umbrella inside	Whistle inside
Wish on a star	Wish on a wishbone	☐	Wish on a star	Wish on a wishbone
Solar eclipse	Lunar eclipse	☐	Solar eclipse	Lunar eclipse
Unicorn	Fairy	☐	Unicorn	Fairy
Itchy palm	Ringing ears	☐	Itchy palm	Ringing ears
Dream of falling	Spilled milk	☐	Dream of falling	Spilled milk
Find a penny	Find a feather	☐	Find a penny	Find a feather
Rain on wedding day	Catch bouquet	☐	Rain on wedding day	Catch bouquet
Hawk sighting	Dolphin sighting	☐	Hawk sighting	Dolphin sighting
Coin in wishing well	Coin in fountain	☐	Coin in wishing well	Coin in fountain
Bird in house	Spider in house	☐	Bird in house	Spider in house
Wish on a star	B-day candles wish	☐	Wish on a star	B-day candles wish
Rainbow	Shooting star	☐	Rainbow	Shooting star

TOTAL MATCHED —— ☐   Get to know each other better! Go to page 122.

CHAPTER 8

SERIOUS STUFF

Fun and games are all well and good, but life's full of serious and important stuff too. In this chapter, you'll cover topics like self-care, religion, money, and politics. You're guaranteed to learn something new and fascinating about your fellow players.

Don't hold back!

HOLD CLOSE TO YOUR
BELIEFS—THEY ARE YOUR
HEART'S COMPASS.

COMMUNICATION

PLAYER 1	MARK X IF	PLAYER 2
Guess Player 2's answers	**MATCHED** ▼	**Fill in your answers!**

PLAYER 1			PLAYER 2	
Texting	Calling	☐	Texting	Calling
Emojis	Words	☐	Emojis	Words
Short and sweet	Long and detailed	☐	Short and sweet	Long and detailed
Email	In-person	☐	Email	In-person
Direct	Indirect	☐	Direct	Indirect
Polite	Straightforward	☐	Polite	Straightforward
Formal	Casual	☐	Formal	Casual
Face to face	Video chat	☐	Face to face	Video chat
Sarcasm	Sincerity	☐	Sarcasm	Sincerity
Exclamation points	Periods	☐	Exclamation points	Periods
Emojis	GIFs	☐	Emojis	GIFs
Funny	Serious	☐	Funny	Serious
Debate	Smile and nod	☐	Debate	Smile and nod
Slang	Formal language	☐	Slang	Formal language
Interrupting	Waiting your turn	☐	Interrupting	Waiting your turn
Giving advice	Just listening	☐	Giving advice	Just listening
Self-focused	Other-focused	☐	Self-focused	Other-focused
Hem and haw	Out with it	☐	Hem and haw	Out with it
Diplomatic	Frank	☐	Diplomatic	Frank
Assertive	Passive	☐	Assertive	Passive

TOTAL MATCHED — ☐

Get to know each other better! Go to page 123.

HOME

PLAYER 2		MARK X IF MATCHED	PLAYER 1	
Fill in your answers!			**Guess Player 2's answers**	
Funky abstract art	Photos everywhere	☐	Funky abstract art	Photos everywhere
Flea market flips	Modern furniture	☐	Flea market flips	Modern furniture
Statement wallpaper	White walls	☐	Statement wallpaper	White walls
Hardwood floors	Shag carpeting	☐	Hardwood floors	Shag carpeting
Indoor plants	Faux plants	☐	Indoor plants	Faux plants
Light and bright	Dark and cozy	☐	Light and bright	Dark and cozy
Neat	Messy	☐	Neat	Messy
Bold patterns	Solid colors	☐	Bold patterns	Solid colors
Coastal calm	Urban oasis	☐	Coastal calm	Urban oasis
Old house	New construction	☐	Old house	New construction
Big yard	Big basement	☐	Big yard	Big basement
Game room	Craft room	☐	Game room	Craft room
Beach cottage	Lake house	☐	Beach cottage	Lake house
Vegetable garden	Flower garden	☐	Vegetable garden	Flower garden
Cat	Dog	☐	Cat	Dog
Suburban street	Downtown	☐	Suburban street	Downtown
Minimalist	Maximalist	☐	Minimalist	Maximalist
Big kitchen	Big bathroom	☐	Big kitchen	Big bathroom
Okay but affordable	Awesome but pricey	☐	Okay but affordable	Awesome but pricey
Where you grew up	Somewhere far away	☐	Where you grew up	Somewhere far away

TOTAL MATCHED ⬚

Get to know each other better! Go to page 123.

CAREER

	PLAYER 1 Guess Player 2's answers	MARK **X** IF MATCHED ▼	PLAYER 2 Fill in your answers!	
Office	Outdoor	☐	Office	Outdoor
Work from home	Work in an office	☐	Work from home	Work in an office
High salary	Passion	☐	High salary	Passion
Traveling	Staying in one place	☐	Traveling	Staying in one place
Creativity	Analytical skills	☐	Creativity	Analytical skills
Physical labor	Mental labor	☐	Physical labor	Mental labor
Helping people	Making money	☐	Helping people	Making money
Teamwork	Working alone	☐	Teamwork	Working alone
Public speaking	Writing	☐	Public speaking	Writing
Lots of meetings	Few meetings	☐	Lots of meetings	Few meetings
Self-employed	Employee	☐	Self-employed	Employee
Lots of benefits	Lots of flexibility	☐	Lots of benefits	Lots of flexibility
Constant learning	Minimal learning	☐	Constant learning	Minimal learning
Hands-on work	Use a computer	☐	Hands-on work	Use a computer
Arts	Sciences	☐	Arts	Sciences
Big city	Small town	☐	Big city	Small town
High demand	Unique position	☐	High demand	Unique position
Startup	Established company	☐	Startup	Established company
Lots of free time	Always busy	☐	Lots of free time	Always busy
Manager	Less responsibility	☐	Manager	Less responsibility

TOTAL MATCHED ☐

Get to know each other better! Go to page 123.

RELIGION & SPIRITUALITY

PLAYER 2	MARK **X** IF	PLAYER 1
Fill in your answers!	MATCHED ▼	Guess Player 2's answers

	PLAYER 2	MARK X IF MATCHED	PLAYER 1	
Religion	Spirituality	☐	Religion	Spirituality
Church	Nature	☐	Church	Nature
Affirmations	Scripture	☐	Affirmations	Scripture
Chanting	Singing	☐	Chanting	Singing
One life	Many lives	☐	One life	Many lives
Meditation	Prayer	☐	Meditation	Prayer
Energy healing	Faith healing	☐	Energy healing	Faith healing
Religious symbols	Crystals	☐	Religious symbols	Crystals
Yoga	Sacred dance	☐	Yoga	Sacred dance
Grace	Karma	☐	Grace	Karma
Monotheism	Polytheism	☐	Monotheism	Polytheism
Creationism	Evolution	☐	Creationism	Evolution
Eastern	Western	☐	Eastern	Western
Candle lighting	Saying a prayer	☐	Candle lighting	Saying a prayer
Forgiveness	Retribution	☐	Forgiveness	Retribution
Private worship	Group worship	☐	Private worship	Group worship
Classic service	Modern service	☐	Classic service	Modern service
Share your beliefs	Keep them private	☐	Share your beliefs	Keep them private
Exploring faiths	Family's faith	☐	Exploring faiths	Family's faith
High priority	Not a priority	☐	High priority	Not a priority

TOTAL MATCHED — ☐

Get to know each other better! Go to page 123.

MONEY

PLAYER 1		MARK **X** IF MATCHED ▼	PLAYER 2	
Guess Player 2's answers			**Fill in your answers!**	
Cash	Venmo	☐	Cash	Venmo
Thrift store	Department store	☐	Thrift store	Department store
Budget	No budget	☐	Budget	No budget
Buy car	Lease car	☐	Buy car	Lease car
Restaurant lunch	Packed lunch	☐	Restaurant lunch	Packed lunch
Shop sales rack	Shop newest stuff	☐	Shop sales rack	Shop newest stuff
Impulse purchases	Planned purchases	☐	Impulse purchases	Planned purchases
Buy cheap	Invest in expensive	☐	Buy cheap	Invest in expensive
Fancy car	Fuel-efficient car	☐	Fancy car	Fuel-efficient car
College savings	Travel fund	☐	College savings	Travel fund
Own a business	Work for others	☐	Own a business	Work for others
Coupon code	Can't be bothered	☐	Coupon code	Can't be bothered
Rich but stressed	Comfy but happy	☐	Rich but stressed	Comfy but happy
Big paycheck	No debt	☐	Big paycheck	No debt
Donate to charity	Give to family	☐	Donate to charity	Give to family
Pick up the check	Leave the tip	☐	Pick up the check	Leave the tip
Shop for yourself	Shop for others	☐	Shop for yourself	Shop for others
Pay bills early	Carry a balance	☐	Pay bills early	Carry a balance
Tip for coffee	Just pay the total	☐	Tip for coffee	Just pay the total
Cryptocurrency	NFTs	☐	Cryptocurrency	NFTs

TOTAL MATCHED — ☐

Get to know each other better! Go to page 123.

SELF-CARE

<table>
<tr>
<td colspan="2">PLAYER 2
Fill in your answers!</td>
<td>MARK X IF
MATCHED
▼</td>
<td colspan="2">PLAYER 1
Guess Player 2's answers</td>
</tr>
</table>

Player 2		Match	Player 1	
Yoga	Meditation	☐	Yoga	Meditation
Face mask	Bubble bath	☐	Face mask	Bubble bath
Therapist	Life coach	☐	Therapist	Life coach
Dance party	Karaoke	☐	Dance party	Karaoke
Head massage	Foot massage	☐	Head massage	Foot massage
Netflix binge	Game night	☐	Netflix binge	Game night
Acupuncture	Reiki	☐	Acupuncture	Reiki
Hike	Bike ride	☐	Hike	Bike ride
Spa service	Afternoon nap	☐	Spa service	Afternoon nap
Green juice	Latte	☐	Green juice	Latte
Art therapy	Music therapy	☐	Art therapy	Music therapy
Park picnic	Brunch with buds	☐	Park picnic	Brunch with buds
Healthy meal	Favorite treat	☐	Healthy meal	Favorite treat
Aromatherapy	Sound healing	☐	Aromatherapy	Sound healing
New book	Old favorite	☐	New book	Old favorite
Forest bathing	Stargazing	☐	Forest bathing	Stargazing
Staycation	Weekend getaway	☐	Staycation	Weekend getaway
Date night	Time alone	☐	Date night	Time alone
Exercise	Rest	☐	Exercise	Rest
Take vitamins	At-home facial	☐	Take vitamins	At-home facial

TOTAL MATCHED ▭

Get to know each other better! Go to page 123.

RELAXATION

	PLAYER 1 Guess Player 2's answers		MARK **X** IF MATCHED ▼		PLAYER 2 Fill in your answers!	

PLAYER 1		MARK X IF MATCHED	PLAYER 2	
Reading	Napping	☐	Reading	Napping
Spa day	Beach day	☐	Spa day	Beach day
Massage roller	Scalp massager	☐	Massage roller	Scalp massager
Go for a drive	Go for a ride	☐	Go for a drive	Go for a ride
Journaling	Coloring	☐	Journaling	Coloring
Nature walk	Sunbathing	☐	Nature walk	Sunbathing
Massage	Acupuncture	☐	Massage	Acupuncture
Hot springs	Sauna	☐	Hot springs	Sauna
Pilates	Tai Chi	☐	Pilates	Tai Chi
Knitting	Crocheting	☐	Knitting	Crocheting
Tea tasting	Coffee tasting	☐	Tea tasting	Coffee tasting
Stargazing	Cloud watching	☐	Stargazing	Cloud watching
Hammock	Swing	☐	Hammock	Swing
Calligraphy	Hand lettering	☐	Calligraphy	Hand lettering
DIY home spa	DIY home décor	☐	DIY home spa	DIY home décor
Outdoor garden	Houseplants	☐	Outdoor garden	Houseplants
Light a candle	Light incense	☐	Light a candle	Light incense
Walk	Jog	☐	Walk	Jog
Mindfulness	Gratitude	☐	Mindfulness	Gratitude
Ambient music	Chill beats	☐	Ambient music	Chill beats

TOTAL MATCHED ☐

Get to know each other better! Go to page 123.

POLITICS

PLAYER 2 — Fill in your answers!		MARK X IF MATCHED ▼	PLAYER 1 — Guess Player 2's answers	
Democrat	Republican	☐	Democrat	Republican
Independent	Libertarian	☐	Independent	Libertarian
World focus	Local focus	☐	World focus	Local focus
Pacifism	Righteous conflict	☐	Pacifism	Righteous conflict
Class mobility	Community identity	☐	Class mobility	Community identity
Corporate freedom	Corporate regulation	☐	Corporate freedom	Corporate regulation
Free market	Regulated market	☐	Free market	Regulated market
Inheritance tax	Free inheritance	☐	Inheritance tax	Free inheritance
Respect authority	Question authority	☐	Respect authority	Question authority
Profit	Ethics	☐	Profit	Ethics
Lower taxes	Higher taxes	☐	Lower taxes	Higher taxes
Local laws	Federal laws	☐	Local laws	Federal laws
Protect the young	Protect the old	☐	Protect the young	Protect the old
Respect the past	Look to the future	☐	Respect the past	Look to the future
Public schools	Private schools	☐	Public schools	Private schools
Subsidize farms	Subsidize medicine	☐	Subsidize farms	Subsidize medicine
Regulate drugs	Outlaw drugs	☐	Regulate drugs	Outlaw drugs
Ample sick leave	Lots of vacation	☐	Ample sick leave	Lots of vacation
Closed borders	Open borders	☐	Closed borders	Open borders
Modernization	Tradition	☐	Modernization	Tradition

TOTAL MATCHED — ☐

Get to know each other better! Go to page 123.

CHAPTER 9

PEOPLE & RELATIONSHIPS

Have you ever wondered which pet peeves drive your fellow players crazy, who believes in one soulmate or multiple loves, which people everyone looks up to as heroes, or whether the players prefer optimistic friends or realistic friends? Well, in this chapter, you'll find out all this and more.

What will you learn about your relationships?

SURROUND YOURSELF WITH
PEOPLE WHO MAKE YOUR
CHEEKS HURT FROM SMILING.

FRIENDS

PLAYER 1	MARK **X** IF	PLAYER 2
Guess Player 2's answers	MATCHED ▼	**Fill in your answers!**

PLAYER 1			PLAYER 2	
Funny	Smart	☐	Funny	Smart
Ambitious	Spontaneous	☐	Ambitious	Spontaneous
Leader	Follower	☐	Leader	Follower
Naughty	Nice	☐	Naughty	Nice
Talker	Listener	☐	Talker	Listener
Ambitious	Easygoing	☐	Ambitious	Easygoing
Calls you out	Keeps quiet	☐	Calls you out	Keeps quiet
Athletic	Artsy	☐	Athletic	Artsy
Optimist	Realist	☐	Optimist	Realist
Supportive	Challenging	☐	Supportive	Challenging
Fashionable	Comfortable	☐	Fashionable	Comfortable
Caring	Funny	☐	Caring	Funny
Cool	Confident	☐	Cool	Confident
Dances	DJs	☐	Dances	DJs
Group friend	Bestie	☐	Group friend	Bestie
Hang at home	Go out together	☐	Hang at home	Go out together
Your house	Their house	☐	Your house	Their house
Crafty	Courageous	☐	Crafty	Courageous
Early	Late	☐	Early	Late
Dog lover	Cat lover	☐	Dog lover	Cat lover

TOTAL MATCHED — ☐

Get to know each other better! Go to page 124.

FAMILY

PLAYER 2 Fill in your answers!		MARK X IF MATCHED ▼	PLAYER 1 Guess Player 2's answers	
Golden child	Black sheep	☐	Golden child	Black sheep
Hang with mom	Hang with dad	☐	Hang with mom	Hang with dad
Share a bedroom	Share a bathroom	☐	Share a bedroom	Share a bathroom
Movies together	Everyone streaming	☐	Movies together	Everyone streaming
Dinner together	Dinner on the run	☐	Dinner together	Dinner on the run
Loud family	Quiet family	☐	Loud family	Quiet family
Dinner at home	Dinner out	☐	Dinner at home	Dinner out
Strict parenting	Lenient parenting	☐	Strict parenting	Lenient parenting
Big family holidays	Intimate gatherings	☐	Big family holidays	Intimate gatherings
Formal dinner	Backyard barbecue	☐	Formal dinner	Backyard barbecue
Formal family photo	Funny selfies	☐	Formal family photo	Funny selfies
Funny family	Serious family	☐	Funny family	Serious family
Early curfew	Late curfew	☐	Early curfew	Late curfew
Kids can drive	Kids get driven	☐	Kids can drive	Kids get driven
Specific chores	Everyone does it all	☐	Specific chores	Everyone does it all
Quiet hours	Chaos	☐	Quiet hours	Chaos
Individual calendars	Family calendar	☐	Individual calendars	Family calendar
Some formal rooms	Every room is lively	☐	Some formal rooms	Every room is lively
Snacks any time	Food at meals only	☐	Snacks any time	Food at meals only
Both parents work	One parent works	☐	Both parents work	One parent works

TOTAL MATCHED ☐

Get to know each other better! Go to page 124.

EVERYDAY HEROES

PLAYER 1	MARK **X** IF MATCHED	PLAYER 2
Guess Player 2's answers	▼	**Fill in your answers!**

PLAYER 1			PLAYER 2	
Firefighter	Police officer	☐	Firefighter	Police officer
Doctor	Nurse	☐	Doctor	Nurse
Teacher	Social worker	☐	Teacher	Social worker
Scientist	Inventor	☐	Scientist	Inventor
Astronaut	Pilot	☐	Astronaut	Pilot
Humanitarian	Activist	☐	Humanitarian	Activist
Environmentalist	Animal rights champ	☐	Environmentalist	Animal rights champ
Entrepreneur	Sports champion	☐	Entrepreneur	Sports champion
Military veteran	War correspondent	☐	Military veteran	War correspondent
Olympic athlete	Famous dancer	☐	Olympic athlete	Famous dancer
Musician	Artist	☐	Musician	Artist
Actor	Director	☐	Actor	Director
Writer	Poet	☐	Writer	Poet
Painter	Photographer	☐	Painter	Photographer
Chef	Baker	☐	Chef	Baker
Fashion designer	Graphic designer	☐	Fashion designer	Graphic designer
Engineer	Architect	☐	Engineer	Architect
Political leader	Online influencer	☐	Political leader	Online influencer
Lawyer	Judge	☐	Lawyer	Judge
Veterinarian	Farmer	☐	Veterinarian	Farmer

TOTAL MATCHED ⬜

Get to know each other better! Go to page 124.

CELEBRITIES

PLAYER 2 — Fill in your answers!		MARK **X** IF MATCHED ▼	PLAYER 1 — Guess Player 2's answers	
Britney Spears	Beyoncé	☐	Britney Spears	Beyoncé
Leonardo DiCaprio	Brad Pitt	☐	Leonardo DiCaprio	Brad Pitt
Justin Timberlake	Justin Bieber	☐	Justin Timberlake	Justin Bieber
Jennifer Aniston	Sandra Bullock	☐	Jennifer Aniston	Sandra Bullock
Tina Fey	Amy Poehler	☐	Tina Fey	Amy Poehler
Rihanna	Lady Gaga	☐	Rihanna	Lady Gaga
Chris Evans	The Rock	☐	Chris Evans	The Rock
Scarlett Johansson	Emma Stone	☐	Scarlett Johansson	Emma Stone
Michelle Obama	Oprah	☐	Michelle Obama	Oprah
Taylor Swift	Katy Perry	☐	Taylor Swift	Katy Perry
Tom Cruise	Harrison Ford	☐	Tom Cruise	Harrison Ford
Jennifer Lawrence	Jennifer Lopez	☐	Jennifer Lawrence	Jennifer Lopez
Jimmy Fallon	Jimmy Kimmel	☐	Jimmy Fallon	Jimmy Kimmel
Meghan Markle	Kate Middleton	☐	Meghan Markle	Kate Middleton
Gordon Ramsay	Rachael Ray	☐	Gordon Ramsay	Rachael Ray
Neil deGrasse Tyson	Bill Nye	☐	Neil deGrasse Tyson	Bill Nye
Adele	Ed Sheeran	☐	Adele	Ed Sheeran
Ben Affleck	Casey Affleck	☐	Ben Affleck	Casey Affleck
Rick Riordan	Stephen King	☐	Rick Riordan	Stephen King
MrBeast	Jacksepticeye	☐	MrBeast	Jacksepticeye

TOTAL MATCHED ⬜

Get to know each other better! Go to page 124.

PARTNER CHARACTER TRAITS

PLAYER 1 Guess Player 2's answers	MARK X IF MATCHED ▼	PLAYER 2 Fill in your answers!
Good-looking · Kindhearted	☐	Good-looking · Kindhearted
Successful · Intelligent	☐	Successful · Intelligent
Open-minded · Opinionated	☐	Open-minded · Opinionated
Spontaneous · Planner	☐	Spontaneous · Planner
Artistic · Scientific	☐	Artistic · Scientific
Physically fit · Hilarious	☐	Physically fit · Hilarious
Sensitive · Thick-skinned	☐	Sensitive · Thick-skinned
Attentive · Laid-back	☐	Attentive · Laid-back
Dreamer · Realist	☐	Dreamer · Realist
Playful · Serious	☐	Playful · Serious
Book-smart · Street-smart	☐	Book-smart · Street-smart
Conservative · Liberal	☐	Conservative · Liberal
Leader · Follower	☐	Leader · Follower
Social · Solitary	☐	Social · Solitary
Outspoken · Reserved	☐	Outspoken · Reserved
Adventurous · Comfort-seeking	☐	Adventurous · Comfort-seeking
Sporty · Academic	☐	Sporty · Academic
Big family · Small family	☐	Big family · Small family
Traveler · Homebody	☐	Traveler · Homebody
Loves to cook · Loves to clean	☐	Loves to cook · Loves to clean

TOTAL MATCHED — ☐

Get to know each other better! Go to page 124.

DATE IDEAS

<table>
<tr><td colspan="2">PLAYER 2
Fill in your answers!</td><td>MARK X IF
MATCHED
▼</td><td colspan="2">PLAYER 1
Guess Player 2's answers</td></tr>
<tr><td>Dinner and a movie</td><td>Picnic</td><td>☐</td><td>Dinner and a movie</td><td>Picnic</td></tr>
<tr><td>Beach sunset</td><td>City skyline view</td><td>☐</td><td>Beach sunset</td><td>City skyline view</td></tr>
<tr><td>Karaoke night</td><td>Board game night</td><td>☐</td><td>Karaoke night</td><td>Board game night</td></tr>
<tr><td>Cooking together</td><td>Going out to eat</td><td>☐</td><td>Cooking together</td><td>Going out to eat</td></tr>
<tr><td>Hiking</td><td>Biking</td><td>☐</td><td>Hiking</td><td>Biking</td></tr>
<tr><td>Concert</td><td>Comedy show</td><td>☐</td><td>Concert</td><td>Comedy show</td></tr>
<tr><td>Ice skating</td><td>Roller skating</td><td>☐</td><td>Ice skating</td><td>Roller skating</td></tr>
<tr><td>Mini-golf</td><td>Bowling</td><td>☐</td><td>Mini-golf</td><td>Bowling</td></tr>
<tr><td>Brunch date</td><td>Dinner date</td><td>☐</td><td>Brunch date</td><td>Dinner date</td></tr>
<tr><td>Swimming</td><td>Thrifting</td><td>☐</td><td>Swimming</td><td>Thrifting</td></tr>
<tr><td>Farmer's market</td><td>Flea market</td><td>☐</td><td>Farmer's market</td><td>Flea market</td></tr>
<tr><td>Horseback riding</td><td>Kayaking</td><td>☐</td><td>Horseback riding</td><td>Kayaking</td></tr>
<tr><td>Art exhibit</td><td>Science museum</td><td>☐</td><td>Art exhibit</td><td>Science museum</td></tr>
<tr><td>Bookstore</td><td>Adventure park</td><td>☐</td><td>Bookstore</td><td>Adventure park</td></tr>
<tr><td>Food truck</td><td>Fancy restaurant</td><td>☐</td><td>Food truck</td><td>Fancy restaurant</td></tr>
<tr><td>Escape room</td><td>Street fair</td><td>☐</td><td>Escape room</td><td>Street fair</td></tr>
<tr><td>Laser tag</td><td>Paintball</td><td>☐</td><td>Laser tag</td><td>Paintball</td></tr>
<tr><td>Arcade</td><td>Theme park</td><td>☐</td><td>Arcade</td><td>Theme park</td></tr>
<tr><td>Double date</td><td>Single date</td><td>☐</td><td>Double date</td><td>Single date</td></tr>
<tr><td>Scenic drive</td><td>Carnival</td><td>☐</td><td>Scenic drive</td><td>Carnival</td></tr>
</table>

TOTAL MATCHED ☐

Get to know each other better! Go to page 124.

ROMANCE

PLAYER 1	MARK **X** IF	PLAYER 2
Guess Player 2's answers	MATCHED ▼	Fill in your answers!

Player 1			Player 2	
Date	Marry	☐	Date	Marry
Love letter	Love song	☐	Love letter	Love song
Flirt	Play it cool	☐	Flirt	Play it cool
Send the text	Wait to be texted	☐	Send the text	Wait to be texted
Flowers	Chocolates	☐	Flowers	Chocolates
Dinner out	Movie night in	☐	Dinner out	Movie night in
Serenade	Poetry	☐	Serenade	Poetry
First date alone	Double date	☐	First date alone	Double date
Holding hands	Hugging	☐	Holding hands	Hugging
Public displays	Private moments	☐	Public displays	Private moments
Good-morning text	Goodnight text	☐	Good-morning text	Goodnight text
Long distance	Close proximity	☐	Long distance	Close proximity
Love grows slowly	Lovestruck instantly	☐	Love grows slowly	Lovestruck instantly
Slow dance	Fast dance	☐	Slow dance	Fast dance
Love note	Love text	☐	Love note	Love text
Romantic picnic	Romantic walk	☐	Romantic picnic	Romantic walk
Opposites attract	Peas in a pod	☐	Opposites attract	Peas in a pod
Meet the family	Meet the friends	☐	Meet the family	Meet the friends
Dating app	Leave to chance	☐	Dating app	Leave to chance
One soulmate	Multiple loves	☐	One soulmate	Multiple loves

TOTAL MATCHED ☐

Get to know each other better! Go to page 124.

PET PEEVES

PLAYER 2 Fill in your answers!		MARK X IF MATCHED ▼	PLAYER 1 Guess Player 2's answers	
Loud chewer	Nail biter	☐	Loud chewer	Nail biter
Interrupting	Ignoring	☐	Interrupting	Ignoring
Glued to phone	Plays loud music	☐	Glued to phone	Plays loud music
Complaining	Bragging	☐	Complaining	Bragging
Latecomer	Oversharer	☐	Latecomer	Oversharer
Backseat driver	Fast driver	☐	Backseat driver	Fast driver
Wastes food	Doesn't recycle	☐	Wastes food	Doesn't recycle
Gum smacking	Whistling	☐	Gum smacking	Whistling
Leaving dishes	Leaving laundry	☐	Leaving dishes	Leaving laundry
One-upping	Name-dropping	☐	One-upping	Name-dropping
Being flaky	Being pushy	☐	Being flaky	Being pushy
Being arrogant	Being rude	☐	Being arrogant	Being rude
Bad parking	Tailgating	☐	Bad parking	Tailgating
Tons of slang	Improper grammar	☐	Tons of slang	Improper grammar
Too serious	Too silly	☐	Too serious	Too silly
Constant texter	Ignores texts	☐	Constant texter	Ignores texts
Poor hygiene	Poor manners	☐	Poor hygiene	Poor manners
Invades space	Won't stop staring	☐	Invades space	Won't stop staring
Indecisive	Aggressive	☐	Indecisive	Aggressive
Smoking	Picky eater	☐	Smoking	Picky eater

TOTAL MATCHED ☐

Get to know each other better! Go to page 124.

CHAPTER 10

GRAB BAG

Turn to this chapter when you're feeling whimsical—it's chock-full of fun and interesting topics to cover with your fellow players. Which grosses you out more: body odor or bad breath? Which trend needs to die: galaxy print or head-to-toe camo? What's your fast-food fave: nachos or loaded fries?

Find out what's in store!

SOMETIMES LIFE IS LIKE
A SURPRISE PARTY—SO
EXPECT THE UNEXPECTED!

TOTALLY GROSS

PLAYER 1 — Guess Player 2's answers	MARK X IF MATCHED ▼	PLAYER 2 — Fill in your answers!
Sour milk · Rotten apples	☐	Sour milk · Rotten apples
Dandruff · Greasy hair	☐	Dandruff · Greasy hair
Tooth cavity · Chipped tooth	☐	Tooth cavity · Chipped tooth
Body odor · Bad breath	☐	Body odor · Bad breath
Dirty dishes · Dirty laundry	☐	Dirty dishes · Dirty laundry
Stale bread · Moldy cheese	☐	Stale bread · Moldy cheese
Sticky hands · Dirty clothes	☐	Sticky hands · Dirty clothes
Dry skin · Chapped lips	☐	Dry skin · Chapped lips
Broken nail · Blister	☐	Broken nail · Blister
Acne · Cold sore	☐	Acne · Cold sore
Splinter · Paper cut	☐	Splinter · Paper cut
Dirty keyboard · Dirty phone screen	☐	Dirty keyboard · Dirty phone screen
Bad haircut · Bad tan lines	☐	Bad haircut · Bad tan lines
Sticky floor · Sticky countertop	☐	Sticky floor · Sticky countertop
Pimple · Mosquito bite	☐	Pimple · Mosquito bite
Coughing · Sneezing	☐	Coughing · Sneezing
Wet socks · Wet hair	☐	Wet socks · Wet hair
Smelly shoes · Smelly locker	☐	Smelly shoes · Smelly locker
Dirty fingernails · Dirty toenails	☐	Dirty fingernails · Dirty toenails
Dead bug · Live bug	☐	Dead bug · Live bug

TOTAL MATCHED —— ☐

Get to know each other better! Go to page 125.

ANIMALS

PLAYER 2 — Fill in your answers!		MARK **X** IF MATCHED ▼	PLAYER 1 — Guess Player 2's answers	
Puppies	Kittens	☐	Puppies	Kittens
Rabbits	Guinea pigs	☐	Rabbits	Guinea pigs
Hamsters	Mice	☐	Hamsters	Mice
Pandas	Koalas	☐	Pandas	Koalas
Dolphins	Whales	☐	Dolphins	Whales
Birds	Fish	☐	Birds	Fish
Hedgehogs	Porcupines	☐	Hedgehogs	Porcupines
Elephants	Giraffes	☐	Elephants	Giraffes
Turtles	Lizards	☐	Turtles	Lizards
Penguins	Seals	☐	Penguins	Seals
Monkeys	Lemurs	☐	Monkeys	Lemurs
Snakes	Spiders	☐	Snakes	Spiders
Otters	Beavers	☐	Otters	Beavers
Tigers	Lions	☐	Tigers	Lions
Chinchillas	Ferrets	☐	Chinchillas	Ferrets
Flamingos	Swans	☐	Flamingos	Swans
Zebras	Horses	☐	Zebras	Horses
Rats	Geckos	☐	Rats	Geckos
Alpacas	Llamas	☐	Alpacas	Llamas
Meerkats	Prairie dogs	☐	Meerkats	Prairie dogs

TOTAL MATCHED ⎯ ☐

Get to know each other better! Go to page 125.

COFFEE, ETC.

PLAYER 1		MARK **X** IF	PLAYER 2	
Guess Player 2's answers		**MATCHED** ▼	**Fill in your answers!**	
Hot chocolate	Chai latte	☐	Hot chocolate	Chai latte
Cappuccino	Latte	☐	Cappuccino	Latte
Tea	Coffee	☐	Tea	Coffee
Americano	Espresso	☐	Americano	Espresso
Hot apple cider	Pumpkin spice latte	☐	Hot apple cider	Pumpkin spice latte
Peppermint mocha	Caramel macchiato	☐	Peppermint mocha	Caramel macchiato
Earl Grey tea	Green tea latte	☐	Earl Grey tea	Green tea latte
Mocha	White hot chocolate	☐	Mocha	White hot chocolate
Matcha latte	Golden milk	☐	Matcha latte	Golden milk
London fog	Black tea	☐	London fog	Black tea
Dunkin'	Starbucks	☐	Dunkin'	Starbucks
Hot chai cider	Spiced apple cider	☐	Hot chai cider	Spiced apple cider
Hot lemon water	Hot honey lemonade	☐	Hot lemon water	Hot honey lemonade
Whipped cream	No whipped cream	☐	Whipped cream	No whipped cream
Packet hot cocoa	Melted hot cocoa	☐	Packet hot cocoa	Melted hot cocoa
Almond milk	Oat milk	☐	Almond milk	Oat milk
Warm eggnog	Gingerbread latte	☐	Warm eggnog	Gingerbread latte
Hot peppermint tea	Hot chamomile tea	☐	Hot peppermint tea	Hot chamomile tea
Coffee with sugar	Coffee without sugar	☐	Coffee with sugar	Coffee without sugar
Tea with milk	Tea with sugar	☐	Tea with milk	Tea with sugar

TOTAL MATCHED ___ ☐

Get to know each other better! Go to page 125.

DATED TRENDS

PLAYER 2 Fill in your answers!		MARK **X** IF MATCHED ▼	PLAYER 1 Guess Player 2's answers	
Shoulder pads	Leg warmers	☐	Shoulder pads	Leg warmers
Bell-bottoms	Parachute pants	☐	Bell-bottoms	Parachute pants
Platform shoes	Crocs	☐	Platform shoes	Crocs
Leisure suits	Flared pantsuits	☐	Leisure suits	Flared pantsuits
Shutter shades	Overalls	☐	Shutter shades	Overalls
Mullets	Rattails	☐	Mullets	Rattails
Jumpsuits	Hot pants	☐	Jumpsuits	Hot pants
Scrunchies	Sweatbands	☐	Scrunchies	Sweatbands
Neon colors	Tie-dye	☐	Neon colors	Tie-dye
Permed hair	Feathered hair	☐	Permed hair	Feathered hair
Infinity scarves	Cold-shoulder tops	☐	Infinity scarves	Cold-shoulder tops
Peplum	Ripped jeans	☐	Peplum	Ripped jeans
Low-rise jeans	High-waisted jeans	☐	Low-rise jeans	High-waisted jeans
Galaxy print	Camo print	☐	Galaxy print	Camo print
Jelly sandals	Clogs	☐	Jelly sandals	Clogs
Leopard print	Zebra print	☐	Leopard print	Zebra print
Ponchos	Chain belts	☐	Ponchos	Chain belts
Go-go boots	Fringe	☐	Go-go boots	Fringe
Mood rings	Wrist bands	☐	Mood rings	Wrist bands
Frosted tips	Mutton chops	☐	Frosted tips	Mutton chops

TOTAL MATCHED ____ ☐

Get to know each other better! Go to page 125.

FACT OR FICTION

PLAYER 1		MARK X IF MATCHED	PLAYER 2	
Guess Player 2's answers		▼	**Fill in your answers!**	
Unicorns fact	Unicorns fiction	☐	Unicorns fact	Unicorns fiction
Aliens fact	Aliens fiction	☐	Aliens fact	Aliens fiction
Atlantis fact	Atlantis fiction	☐	Atlantis fact	Atlantis fiction
Bigfoot fact	Bigfoot fiction	☐	Bigfoot fact	Bigfoot fiction
Loch Ness fact	Loch Ness fiction	☐	Loch Ness fact	Loch Ness fiction
Ghosts fact	Ghosts fiction	☐	Ghosts fact	Ghosts fiction
UFOs fact	UFOs fiction	☐	UFOs fact	UFOs fiction
Illuminati fact	Illuminati fiction	☐	Illuminati fact	Illuminati fiction
Time travel fact	Time travel fiction	☐	Time travel fact	Time travel fiction
Mermaids fact	Mermaids fiction	☐	Mermaids fact	Mermaids fiction
Vampires fact	Vampires fiction	☐	Vampires fact	Vampires fiction
Telekinesis fact	Telekinesis fiction	☐	Telekinesis fact	Telekinesis fiction
Mind reading fact	Mind reading fiction	☐	Mind reading fact	Mind reading fiction
Fairies fact	Fairies fiction	☐	Fairies fact	Fairies fiction
Yeti fact	Yeti fiction	☐	Yeti fact	Yeti fiction
Chupacabra fact	Chupacabra fiction	☐	Chupacabra fact	Chupacabra fiction
Witches fact	Witches fiction	☐	Witches fact	Witches fiction
El Dorado fact	El Dorado fiction	☐	El Dorado fact	El Dorado fiction
True AI fact	True AI fiction	☐	True AI fact	True AI fiction
Werewolves fact	Werewolves fiction	☐	Werewolves fact	Werewolves fiction

TOTAL MATCHED ⎯ ☐

Get to know each other better! Go to page 125.

PETS

PLAYER 2 — Fill in your answers!		MARK X IF MATCHED ▼	PLAYER 1 — Guess Player 2's answers	
Dog	Cat	☐	Dog	Cat
Small dog	Big dog	☐	Small dog	Big dog
Golden retriever	Black Labrador	☐	Golden retriever	Black Labrador
Pug	Poodle	☐	Pug	Poodle
German shepherd	Husky	☐	German shepherd	Husky
Chihuahua	Yorkie	☐	Chihuahua	Yorkie
Goldendoodle	Dalmatian	☐	Goldendoodle	Dalmatian
Boxer	Dachshund	☐	Boxer	Dachshund
Corgi	Pomeranian	☐	Corgi	Pomeranian
Turtle	Fish	☐	Turtle	Fish
One pet	Multiple pets	☐	One pet	Multiple pets
Guinea pig	Hamster	☐	Guinea pig	Hamster
Parrot	Hermit crab	☐	Parrot	Hermit crab
Parakeet	Finch	☐	Parakeet	Finch
Frog	Lizard	☐	Frog	Lizard
Chicken	Rabbit	☐	Chicken	Rabbit
Goldfish	Betta fish	☐	Goldfish	Betta fish
Maine coon	Persian	☐	Maine coon	Persian
Siamese	Sphynx	☐	Siamese	Sphynx
Munchkin	Manx	☐	Munchkin	Manx

TOTAL MATCHED ☐

Get to know each other better! Go to page 125.

AWKWARD MOMENTS

PLAYER 1		MARK **X** IF MATCHED ▼	PLAYER 2	
Guess Player 2's answers			Fill in your answers!	
Tripping	Spilling	☐	Tripping	Spilling
Bad breath	Body odor	☐	Bad breath	Body odor
Food in teeth	TP on shoe	☐	Food in teeth	TP on shoe
Accidental text	Accidental dial	☐	Accidental text	Accidental dial
Forgot name	Forgot birthday	☐	Forgot name	Forgot birthday
Bad hair	Outfit mishap	☐	Bad hair	Outfit mishap
Wrong restroom	Wrong pronoun	☐	Wrong restroom	Wrong pronoun
Accidental burp	Loud hiccups	☐	Accidental burp	Loud hiccups
Singing in public	Dancing in public	☐	Singing in public	Dancing in public
Accidental snort	Accidental drool	☐	Accidental snort	Accidental drool
Lip-syncing	Karaoke	☐	Lip-syncing	Karaoke
Voice crack	Loud sneeze	☐	Voice crack	Loud sneeze
Smudged makeup	Sweat stains	☐	Smudged makeup	Sweat stains
Trip in heels	Fall in flip-flops	☐	Trip in heels	Fall in flip-flops
Missed button	Zipper down	☐	Missed button	Zipper down
Bad hair	Bad manners	☐	Bad hair	Bad manners
Sneeze on someone	Cough on someone	☐	Sneeze on someone	Cough on someone
Laughing too loud	Missing the joke	☐	Laughing too loud	Missing the joke
Mismatched socks	Shirt inside out	☐	Mismatched socks	Shirt inside out
Dumb ringtone	Terrible wedgie	☐	Dumb ringtone	Terrible wedgie

TOTAL MATCHED ⎯ ☐

Get to know each other better! Go to page 125.

FAST FOOD

PLAYER 2 — Fill in your answers!		MARK X IF MATCHED ▼	PLAYER 1 — Guess Player 2's answers	
Drive through	Dine in	☐	Drive through	Dine in
Hamburgers	Chicken sandwiches	☐	Hamburgers	Chicken sandwiches
Fried chicken	Grilled chicken	☐	Fried chicken	Grilled chicken
French fries	Onion rings	☐	French fries	Onion rings
Pizza	Tacos	☐	Pizza	Tacos
Burritos	Quesadillas	☐	Burritos	Quesadillas
Hot dogs	Corndogs	☐	Hot dogs	Corndogs
Chicken nuggets	Chicken tenders	☐	Chicken nuggets	Chicken tenders
Grilled cheese	Cheeseburgers	☐	Grilled cheese	Cheeseburgers
Milkshakes	Smoothies	☐	Milkshakes	Smoothies
Soft-serve ice cream	Frozen yogurt	☐	Soft-serve ice cream	Frozen yogurt
Breakfast burritos	Egg sandwiches	☐	Breakfast burritos	Egg sandwiches
Soda	Iced tea	☐	Soda	Iced tea
Nachos	Loaded fries	☐	Nachos	Loaded fries
Onion rings	Mozzarella sticks	☐	Onion rings	Mozzarella sticks
Baked potatoes	Curly fries	☐	Baked potatoes	Curly fries
Fish sandwiches	Fish and chips	☐	Fish sandwiches	Fish and chips
Fried rice	Chow mein	☐	Fried rice	Chow mein
Cheesesteak	Italian sub	☐	Cheesesteak	Italian sub
Meatball sub	Pulled pork sandwich	☐	Meatball sub	Pulled pork sandwich

TOTAL MATCHED ☐

Get to know each other better! Go to page 125.

WOULD YOU RATHER?

Live without the internet or without a car?

Have a personal chef or a personal trainer?

Have unlimited money or infinite wisdom?

Travel back in time or into the future?

WILD CARD!

Make up a question about the future

Find your soulmate or find a million dollars?

Live alone in the woods or on a desert island?

Drink sour milk or eat dog food?

Have great fashion sense or a perfect fitness regimen?

Know how long you'll live or let it remain a mystery?

Use this activity as an icebreaker to get to know friends better or when you're just in the mood to try something new. Choose questions randomly or add an element of surprise by closing your eyes and pointing your finger onto the page to select a mystery question.

Spend a week on a deserted island or in a medieval castle?

WILD CARD!

Make up a question about relationships

Have the ability to fly or to time-travel?

Live in extreme heat or extreme cold?

Eat only ice cream for a year or no ice cream for a year?

WILD CARD!

Make up a question about something silly or gross

Be famous for your philanthropy or your business skills?

Win an Academy Award or win the lottery?

Find true love forever or have a date with your celebrity crush?

Be beautiful or intelligent?

TELL ME MORE

This chapter is your destination if you were unable to accurately predict at least half of your fellow player's answers. But that just means you get to break out of the binary format and ask some meatier questions! Enjoy the conversation.

Flip through to find the questions that go with your chapter and quiz!

THE IMPORTANT THING IS
NOT TO STOP QUESTIONING.
CURIOSITY HAS ITS OWN
REASON FOR EXISTING.

—ALBERT EINSTEIN

TELL ME MORE ◇ HAPPY HOBBIES

14 **MUSIC MANIA**
- What was the first album you purchased?
- What's the best concert you ever attended?
- What is your least favorite genre of music?

15 **HOBBY TIME**
- What hobby do you spend the most time doing?
- What is a hobby you would love to learn?
- Which hobbies do you think are the coolest, but not for you?

16 **ATHLETICS**
- How many sports teams have you played on?
- Who do you know who would make great team members?
- Do you have any sports idols? Who are they?

17 **EXTRACURRICULARS**
- What club do you wish existed in your school or community?
- How many clubs are you involved in (or were way back when)?
- Do you think clubs are important for everyone to try?

18 **TECH & GADGETS**
- Are you generally an early or late adapter of new technology?
- What is the most money you've ever spent on a piece of tech?
- What technology or gadget couldn't you live without?

19 **ENTERTAINMENT**
- How many times in a normal week do you feel bored?
- What is a new activity someone recently introduced you to?
- Do you prefer having fun while sitting or while moving?

20 **SHOPPING**
- What type of item do you spend the most money on?
- What's something cool or interesting you bought recently?
- Have you ever bought something exclusive or limited edition?

21 **OUTDOOR FUN**
- What adventure sport are you dying to try?
- What's your favorite kind of weather for a day outside?
- How much prep time do you need to get ready for outdoor fun?

TELL ME MORE ◇ FOOD & DRINK

24 FOOD FAVES
- What restaurant do you like to go to for celebrations?
- What is your absolute least favorite food?
- What food would you eat every day if you could?

25 BREAKFAST
- Do you have a big appetite right when you wake up?
- What does your go-to weekend breakfast consist of?
- Are you a bigger fan of breakfast or of brunch?

26 LUNCH
- Do you prefer a bigger lunch or a bigger dinner?
- What personal lunch recipe are you super proud of?
- Do you like to eat fast and move on or linger over lunch?

27 DINNER
- What time do you eat dinner on weeknights? Weekends?
- Do you like leftovers or do you leave them for others?
- What does your dream burger (meat or veggie patty!) consist of?

28 DESSERT
- Do you feel guilty when you eat dessert? Why or why not?
- What special holiday dessert do you look forward to all year?
- What is your favorite dessert to bake at home?

29 SIDE DISHES
- How many sides do you like for a solid, well-rounded meal?
- Does your family have rules about going back for seconds?
- What side dish do you wish you never had to eat again?

30 SNACKS
- What's your favorite snack to reach for when you're peckish?
- Which popular snack is a big disappointment to you?
- If you could invent a snack, what ingredients would go into it?

31 BEVERAGES
- Do you reach for real-sugar drinks or diet versions?
- Do you like drinking water? Do you think you drink enough of it?
- Have you ever tasted a drink and immediately spat it out?

TELL ME MORE ◇ ME, MYSELF & I

34 ALL ABOUT ME
- What is the best compliment someone ever gave you?
- What do you think is your biggest personal flaw?
- How would you describe your personality in a dozen words?

35 HABITS
- What's a bad habit that you broke or otherwise overcame?
- What good habit are you trying to develop in your life?
- What do you recommend for building good habits?

36 CHILDHOOD NOSTALGIA
- What from your childhood has recently become popular again?
- What childhood toy or item will you never get rid of?
- What do you miss most from your childhood (or younger years)?

37 SCHOOL
- Are or were you happy to go to school on an average day?
- What is or was your favorite thing about school?
- Have you had an especially memorable or great teacher?

38 FEARS
- Have you ever outgrown a fear or taken steps to face it?
- What fear crops up the most frequently in your daily life?
- What techniques do you use to deal with your fears?

39 STORYBOOK ROLES
- When you picture yourself as a character in a story, who are you?
- Do you generally feel more interested in heroes or villains?
- What story character cliché are you tired of hearing about?

40 CAREER IDEAS
- Do your career dreams require higher education?
- What did you used to want to be when you were younger?
- If you didn't have to worry about money, what job would you do?

41 MY FUTURE
- Can you predict where you'll be in five years? Ten? Twenty?
- How important are career and family to you?
- Have you ever experienced a drastic, unexpected life change?

TELL ME MORE ◈ MEDIA

(44) BOOKS

- What kind of book would you love to write?
- What are the top three books you've ever read?
- What book world would you love to visit?

(45) ART

- What kind (or kinds) of art do you think you are good at?
- Do you notice art in everyday life? Where and when?
- How much would you spend for a painting that you loved?

(46) MOVIES & FILM

- What job would you prefer to have in making a movie?
- What is your all-time favorite movie or movie franchise?
- Who are your favorite actors and actresses?

(47) MOVIE TIME

- How often do you watch a movie in a theater?
- Do you prefer director's cuts or theatrical versions?
- What snack do you wish you could sneak into a movie theater?

(48) SOCIAL MEDIA

- Which social media site do you spend the most time on?
- Which social media site do you enjoy using the most?
- Do you think you have a healthy relationship with social media?

(49) TELEVISION

- What is your all-time favorite television series?
- What is the last television show you completed?
- What story do you wish would be adapted into a show?

(50) VIDEO GAMES

- What is the coolest video game you've ever played?
- What game did you fail to beat, despite your best efforts?
- What game do you think is totally overrated?

(51) BOARD GAMES

- What board game do you always suggest to play?
- Are you best at word games, puzzle games, or something else?
- What board game do you think would be cool as a movie?

TELL ME MORE ◇ STYLE & FASHION

54 **FASHION**
- What category of clothing do you own the most of?
- What's the most you ever spent on a piece of clothing?
- What clothing would you design if you were a fashion designer?

55 **SHOES**
- How many pairs of shoes are in your closet?
- What is the longest you've ever owned a single pair of shoes?
- Have you ever customized your shoes? If so, how?

56 **ACCESSORIES**
- What is your favorite accessory in your closet?
- What is your favorite store (in person or online) to shop at?
- What one kind of accessory couldn't you live without?

57 **HAIR**
- How often do you change up the cut of your hair?
- Have you ever dyed your hair? If so, what colors?
- Is hair a fun way to express yourself or a nuisance to you?

58 **MAKEUP**
- How often do you wear makeup versus go bare faced?
- Do you consider yourself good at doing makeup?
- Is your relationship to makeup positive or complicated?

59 **GROOMING**
- What grooming task feels seemingly never-ending for you?
- Is there a grooming task from the quiz that you'd like to try?
- How long does it take you to get ready on an average day?

60 **JEWELRY**
- Do you own any pieces of jewelry that are heirlooms or special?
- Do you like when people buy you jewelry?
- How many pieces of jewelry do you wear on an average day?

61 **BODY MODS**
- Have you even gotten a piercing? How much did it hurt?
- Do you want any tattoos? What would your next tattoo be?
- Do you think plastic surgery should be easier or harder to get?

TELL ME MORE ◇ THE WORLD

64) DESTINATION CITIES
- What city from the quiz would you love to win a trip to?
- What city or cities from the quiz had you never heard of before?
- What city do you think you'd like to live in or near?

65) SIGHTS TO SEE
- Do you prefer natural sights or elaborate attractions?
- What sight from the quiz are you dying to see some day?
- What are the popular sights in your state or region?

66) COUNTRIES TO VISIT
- If you could explore any country in the world, what would it be?
- Do you speak other languages? How did you learn them?
- Have you ever been to another country? What was it like?

67) INTERNATIONAL CUISINE
- How many foods in the quiz have you tasted in your life?
- What unfamiliar food from the quiz did you have to look up?
- Which of the foods from the quiz do you cook at home?

68) ENVIRONMENT
- What do you do to help protect the environment?
- What do you think is the worst thing for the environment?
- Have you seen environmental changes in your life?

69) NATURE
- Do you consider yourself a nature lover? Why or why not?
- What is the most beautiful natural sight you've ever seen?
- Do you prefer your home climate or somewhere else's?

70) WEATHER
- How much does rain on the weekend bother you?
- What is the most extreme weather you've ever experienced?
- Do you obsessively check the forecast or just roll with it?

71) VACATION
- Have you ever been on a cruise? Does a cruise interest you?
- What is the best vacation you've ever been on?
- What is the worst vacation you've ever suffered through?

TELL ME MORE ◇ FUN STUFF

(74) HOLIDAYS
- What is the most memorable holiday you've ever had?
- What holiday do you wish would come more than once a year?
- What holiday would you create if you had the power?

(75) CARS
- How do you feel about driving and cars in general?
- What kinds of cars have your family owned or used?
- What is your dream car? How would you customize it?

(76) GAME SHOWS
- Do you think you could win a game show? If so, which one?
- Do you play along with any game shows at home?
- Whom would you include in your own epic game show team?

(77) FLOWERS
- Have you ever given or received a bouquet of flowers?
- What kind of flower do you think smells the most heavenly?
- Are you good at identifying different flower species?

(78) DANCE MOVES
- Have you ever taken formal dance classes?
- What kind of dance would you love to learn?
- When did you last absolutely break it down on the dance floor?

(79) SUPERHEROES
- Do you generally like superhero stories? Why or why not?
- What superhero do you personally relate to the most?
- How would you define a superhero versus a regular hero?

(80) TIME TRAVEL
- What single year in the future would you choose to visit?
- Would you time-travel if you had to stay for a full year?
- What time period do you know the most about?

(81) SUPERSTITIONS & LUCK
- Have you ever felt like you did something to earn bad luck?
- Do you believe that people can affect their own luck?
- What superstition do you swear is true—or at least live by?

TELL ME MORE ◈ SERIOUS STUFF

84) COMMUNICATION
- Have you ever completely misunderstood someone? How?
- Do you swear never, rarely, sometimes, or often?
- Have you ever accidentally offended someone?

85) HOME
- What ten words would you use to describe your dream home?
- How similar is your current home to your dream home?
- Would you rather renovate yourself or pay someone to do it?

86) CAREER
- How many hours per week do you think people should work?
- When would you like to retire? When do you think you'll retire?
- How would you describe a perfect workday?

87) RELIGION & SPIRITUALITY
- What makes religion important or not important to you?
- Have you ever gone to a religious service of a different religion?
- In what ways do you express your spirituality?

88) MONEY
- How much of your time do you spend worrying about money?
- Have you ever regretted a big purchase?
- What problems do you think money cannot solve?

89) SELF-CARE
- How often do you engage in self-care activities?
- What unfamiliar activity from the quiz would you like to try?
- Can you help anyone in your life take some time for self-care?

90) RELAXATION
- How many times per week do you do relaxing activities?
- Are there people in your life who are relaxing to be around?
- What unfamiliar activity from the quiz would you like to try?

91) POLITICS
- Are there issues you wish you were better informed about?
- Do any of your opinions differ strongly from friends or family?
- How have you participated in politics in your life?

TELL ME MORE ◇ PEOPLE & RELATIONSHIPS

94 FRIENDS

- Whom have you been friends with the longest?
- Where did you meet the last good friend you made?
- What characteristic do all your friends have in common?

95 FAMILY

- Do you get along easily with your family, or is it a struggle?
- How would you describe your family to a complete stranger?
- What lessons have you learned from your family?

96 EVERYDAY HEROES

- Do you know anyone who has one of the jobs in the quiz?
- Has your life ever been impacted by an everyday hero?
- Have you ever considered any of the quiz jobs as a career?

97 CELEBRITIES

- Do you follow along with any celebrity gossip or websites?
- What celebrity would you love to spend a day with?
- What celebrity are you tired of people talking about?

98 PARTNER CHARACTER TRAITS

- Do you think you have low, high, or perfect standards?
- What is a total deal-breaker in a romantic partner?
- What trait do you look for but don't have yourself?

99 DATE IDEAS

- What is the most memorable date you've been on?
- Have you ever had to turn someone down for a date?
- What is your go-to activity for a first date?

100 ROMANCE

- How do you like to express affection to a romantic partner?
- Who are some positive romantic role models in your life?
- How important is romance in your life right now? In the future?

101 PET PEEVES

- Have you ever left a room or flipped out due to a pet peeve?
- Are you guilty of any of the pet peeves listed in the quiz?
- Do you think any common pet peeves are actually no big deal?

TELL ME MORE ◇ GRAB BAG

104 TOTALLY GROSS
- How many gross experiences from the quiz have you lived?
- Do things easily gross you out or are you chill and stoic?
- Have you ever purposely tried to gross someone out?

105 ANIMALS
- Do you consider yourself an animal lover? Why or why not?
- What species' future are you worried about the most?
- What animal do you wish you had the power to turn into?

106 COFFEE, ETC.
- Are you a coffee drinker? What's your favorite coffee drink?
- Do you enjoy hot drinks during the summer?
- What is your dream hot-beverage recipe? List all the ingredients!

107 DATED TRENDS
- Do you wear any of the trends listed in the quiz?
- Do you have family or friends who love any of the trends?
- Which trend do you hope never sees the light of day again?

108 FACT OR FICTION
- Do you consider yourself to be a gullible person?
- Have you ever believed in a conspiracy?
- What fictional thing from the quiz do you wish was real?

109 PETS
- What one animal would you love to train as your companion?
- How many pets (number and species) do you want to have?
- Do you think everyone should have a pet? Why or why not?

110 AWKWARD MOMENTS
- What is your most embarrassing, let-me-disappear memory?
- Have you ever laughed at someone without meaning to?
- What embarrassing moment do you no longer find cringey?

111 FAST FOOD
- How often do you eat fast food in a month?
- Are you loyal to any fast-food chains? Why or why not?
- What menu item are you chronically unable to resist?

HOW DID IT GO?

Once you have completed this entire book, take a few
minutes to sit down and think about the experience.
You can do this alone or, better yet, with your fellow players.

Who participated in the most games?

_____

_____

_____

_____

_____

Who won the most games?

_____

_____

_____

_____

_____

What was the funniest thing you revealed?

_____

_____

_____

_____

_____

What was the most surprising thing you revealed?

_____

_____

_____

_____

_____

What are the most memorable things you learned?

_____

_____

_____

_____

_____

_____

_____

_____

What were your favorite quizzes?

_____

_____

_____

_____

_____

_____

_____

_____

Which quizzes sparked longer conversations?

_____

_____

_____

_____

_____

_____

_____

_____

Did any quizzes kick off a heated debate?

_____

_____

_____

_____

_____

_____

_____

_____

BETTER DAY BOOKS®

HAPPY · CREATIVE · CURATED

Business is personal at Better Day Books. We were founded on the belief that all people are creative and that making things by hand is inherently good for us. It's important to us that you know how much we appreciate your support. The book you are holding in your hands was crafted with the artistic passion of the author and brought to life by a team of wildly enthusiastic creatives who believed it could inspire you. If it did, please drop us a line and let us know about it. Connect with us on Instagram, post a photo of your art, and let us know what other creative pursuits you are interested in learning about. It all matters to us. You're kind of a big deal.

it's a good day to have a better day!®

www.betterdaybooks.com

better_day_books